About the

ERIC HARRISON was born in the sm
Bridge in 1938. Some years later he fulfill   _.._ o. becoming a professional footballer at his local club, Halifax Town. His career as a journeyman
professional in the lower leagues, firstly with Halifax and then Hartlepool
United, Barrow, Southport and Scarborough, lasted 17 years and encompassed
more than 550 league and cup games.

On his retirement from playing, he joined Everton as youth coach and
in his nine years at Goodison Park rose to become first team coach. In 1981,
the newly installed Manchester United manager, Ron Atkinson, brought Eric
to Old Trafford as Youth Team Manager, a post in which he had an immediate impact, uncovering and nurturing the talent of Mark Hughes and Norman
Whiteside amongst many others.

The replacement of Atkinson with Alex Ferguson in 1986, however,
was to see the beginning of Eric Harrison's most lasting legacy to Manchester
United Football Club. Under the guidance of Ferguson and the tutelage of
Harrison a youth structure was built at Old Trafford which culminated in the
famous 'Class of 92', a group of young players - Ryan Giggs, David Beckham,
Paul Scholes, Nicky Butt and Gary and Phil Neville - who were to become, and
still remain, the nucleus of the Manchester United side which has come to
dominate English football.

THE VIEW FROM THE DUGOUT is Eric Harrison's own story
from those humble beginnings in Hebden Bridge; his playing career; his rise
up the coaching ladder at Everton, and then on to Manchester United and his
part in its current position as one of the finest and most powerful clubs in the
World.

Moreover, in this book Harrison pulls few punches with his outspoken
views on the state of the game in this country and the legacy of mis-manage-
ment of F.A. coaching courses. With his long career at the grassroots, his
wealth of coaching experience at the top level, and his current position in
international football as the assistant to Mark Hughes with Wales, few people
can be as qualified as he to speak about our national sport, its problems and
the solutions. **THE VIEW FROM THE DUGOUT** is essential reading, not
only for fans of Manchester United, but all lovers of the game of football.

THE VIEW FROM THE DUGOUT

The Autobiography of Eric Harrison

Best wishes,

Eric Harrison

WITH A FOREWORD BY SIR ALEX FERGUSON

The Parrs Wood Press
MANCHESTER

First Published 2001

THE PARRS WOOD PRESS
St Wilfrid's Enterprise Centre
Royce Road, Manchester, M15 5BJ

© Eric Harrison 2001

ISBN: 1 903158 16 8

Front cover design by Glenn B. Fleming

This book was produced by Andy Searle, Ruth Heritage and Helen Faulkner of The Parrs Wood Press and Printed in Great Britain by:

MFP Design and Print
Longford Trading Estate
Thomas Street
Stretford
Manchester M32 0JT

CONTENTS

PHOTOGRAPHS

ACKNOWLEDGEMENTS

This book has been a very enjoyable and interestingexperience for me, looking back over my long career in football. It surprised me how much of a team effort it turned out to be - so there are a lot of people to mention.

Firstly, I'd like to thank John Richardson, a football reporter with real enthusiasm, and a good friend. He got the whole idea off the ground and did most of the research. John then led me to Andy Searle and The Parrs Wood Press. I am more than happy that this book has been published in Manchester and I am indebted to Andy and the hard work he and his assistants, Ruth Heritage and Helen Faulkner, have put into the book. My special thanks here, too, go to Brian Halford. Brian is an up-and-coming sports writer currently working for the Birmingham Post. It was he who took the hotchpotch of chapters and ideas and turned it into a coherent record of my life.

Sir Alex Ferguson is the man responsible for the wonderful success at Old Trafford over the last decade and I am grateful to him for his support and friendship and for the kind words he has provided in his Foreword.

Glenn Fleming did the striking cover design, whilst for the photographs that were not out of my private collection I would like to thank John Peters, Manchester United's official photographer, the Liverpool Echo and Everton Football Club. Cliff Butler, the programme editor at United, has given me invaluable help as well.

On a personal note, Shirley, my wife, has been my greatest supporter and I feel lucky to have been blessed with such a wonderful family. I have two lovely daughters, Kim and Vicky, and three gorgeous grandchildren, Ashleigh, Connor and Joseph.

Obviously I would like to extend my best wishes to all players and staff, past and present, with whom I have worked, not only at Manchester United but also at Everton and the clubs I appeared for during my playing career. Without exception everyone I have played and worked with has been fantastic. I would, though, like to give a special mention to Jimmy Curran, my assistant at United for the last 17 years, who has been a loyal and trusted colleague and friend.

I hope you enjoy reading this book.

Eric Harrison
Halifax
February 2001

v

FOREWORD

by Sir Alex Ferguson

First of all I would like to say how delighted I was to receive an invitation to make this small contribution to Eric Harrison's book. During all the years we spent together at Old Trafford he proved to be an exemplary character, a treasured colleague and a first class coach.

In my opinion he is one of the best coaches this country has ever produced, and I think that Manchester United was extremely fortunate to have him in charge of its junior section. His work with young players is legendary in the game, and his remarkable success rate at bringing youngsters through the ranks would indeed take some beating.

Eric was already on the staff when I arrived at Old Trafford in November1986, having been recruited by my predecessor, Ron Atkinson. It was quite a coup on Ron's part to recruit Eric, for at the time he was first team coach at Everton. It was one of the best day's work Ron ever did for Manchester United, because Eric went on to become the best youth coach I have known.

His record in bringing through players such as Mark Hughes, Norman Whiteside, David Beckham, Nicky Butt, Paul Scholes, Gary and Phil Neville - the list goes on - speaks for itself. The priority of any junior coach is to develop players for greater things, with winning trophies being one of the lesser requirements. That may be the case but it didn't stop Eric's teams from collecting numerous Lancashire League titles and a couple of FA Youth Cups.

Eric's time at Old Trafford will always be best remembered for his affinity with the 1992 side, which beat Crystal Palace in the final to win the FA Youth Cup for the first time in 28 years. That team, which became affectionately known as the "Dream Team", contained many of the players I have previously mentioned.

Eric had the knack of getting the very best from young players and perhaps that was because he is a perfectionist himself. I have lost count of the times he has stormed out of the coaches' room at The Cliff at half time, en route for the dressing room, anger and frustration etched on his face. And that was when the team was winning comfortably! It is no wonder that they very rarely lost during his reign at the club.

Eric was a tremendous servant to Manchester United and he played an enormous part in the club's revival during the 1990s. In fact, I would go as far as to say that it is almost impossible to measure his contribution. He is a great professional, a terrific coach, a true friend and above all a smashing fellow.

1.

A lucky man

ONE CRISP EARLY SUMMER EVENING, late in May 1999, inside the magnificent Nou Camp Stadium in Barcelona, Ole Gunnar Solksjaer swept a football from close range into a goal net. It was a simple act which the Norwegian striker had completed many times before. This time, though, it was a bit special.

As the ball settled behind the goal-line, there was a split-second of stunned silence all round the vast, packed stadium. Then came a tidal wave of English noise. Because the goal net in question was that of Bayern Munich. The German club had been leading Manchester United 1-0 as the Champions League final entered injury time. Then Teddy Sheringham equalised and now, in the third and final minute of injury time, Solskjaer, from Sheringham's assist, had made it 2-1. Somehow, from the very brink of defeat, Manchester United had completed one of the most astounding comebacks in the history of football.

They had beaten one of Europe's most accomplished clubs to lift the European Champions League trophy - the European Cup that Sir Matt Busby's wonderful United team had lifted more than 30 years before. By doing so, Sir Alex Ferguson's side had completed a historic treble: the Champions League, the Premiership and the FA

The View From the Dugout

Cup.

Many people on that unforgettable night in Spain were as proud as could be but no-one was prouder or more emotional than myself. Many members of the United squad that had built and completed that phenomenal treble achievement were "my boys." They had come all the way through Manchester United's youth system. Discovered, nurtured, encouraged and improved by the club's coaches and I had been priviliged to be at the helm as they turned from promising boys into true men. Achievers.

That night, as the celebrations really got underway David Beckham, Ryan Giggs, Paul Scholes and the Neville brothers sought me out to share their joy. These players, superstars at the very top of their profession, seeking out Eric Harrison - former wing-half with Hartlepool, Halifax, Barrow, Southport and Scarborough - to say thanks.

How did I feel? Thrilled? Yes. Flattered? Yes. Happy. But more than anything else I thought to myself: what a lucky man.

My career has travelled, as much as any ever could, from one extreme to the other. From sharing a mug of hot bovril to keep out the cold in Halifax Town's dilapidated dressing-room to sipping champagne at the Nou Camp as part of the greatest night in the history of the greatest football club in the world. Oh yes, a lucky, lucky man.

I played all my football - 550 league and cup games - in the lower divisions of the Football League (or just below it). I spent my whole career playing in front of one or two thousand people kicking lumps out of opponents in pursuit of a tiny but oh-so-precious win bonus at the end of the week. If someone had said to me back then, on a frosty night at Halifax's Shay Ground after we had battled through 90 minutes against the likes of Crewe Alexandra or Lincoln City, that I would one day be part of the club that dominates Europe I would have told them to get some therapy. Even Roy of the Rovers stories have their limits.

2

I vividly remember my first contract as a player. I was thrilled to get a deal for one season with Halifax Town. Not much security there but in the 17 years I was to play professional football, I was only ever to get a contract for one season at a time. My first wage was £14 a week in the winter and £12 in the summer - as Tommy Docherty often jokes, footballers must have been bad players in the summer.

Those, of course, were the times of the maximum wage. What a difference these days. When I was in hospital some time ago with a thrombosis in my leg, I could not stop thinking about the doctors and nurses who were saving people's lives yet only earning a fraction of what the top footballers earn. The poor nurses are on a pittance compared to those footballers.

Back in the 1950s and 1960s players' wages were poor but when they started rising they soon made up for lost time. I remember, as far back as 1979, accompanying Everton's chairman Sir Philip Carter on a mission to try to sign Scottish international Asa Hartford. Gordon Lee, the Everton manager, was on holiday, so I had to go with the chairman to meet Asa. The three of us met at a hotel and when Asa told the chairman the terms he wanted, I was stunned. He asked for a fortune and I thought he was having a laugh but Sir Philip told me it was just a normal wage for top First Division players at the time.

Even what Asa wanted is peanuts to what players earn these days. Good luck to today's players. If they can get the money, then fine, but spare a thought for the poor old nurses. Crazy. Still, that's another story.

This is my story and it is the story of a man who is football crazy. Always have been, always will be. I still remember the day I signed as a professional footballer for Halifax. It was the best moment of my football career. I have had some unbelievable moments but that first step - actually achieving what I had always dreamt about as a young boy in desperately wanting to be a footballer

3

The View From the Dugout

- meant everything to me. Every professional footballer should get down on their knees and pray that their dream has come true. They should give 100% all the time in training and in games. Most do - but those that do not should be ashamed of themselves. Me, I was thrilled to bits to be on my way and determined to make the most of whatever talent I had been born with.

2.

Halifax and Hartlepool

AS A BOY GROWING UP IN HEBDEN BRIDGE - a small village in west Yorkshire between Halifax and Burnley - I was, like many boys, football daft.

I lived for the game and during lessons at school my mind was always wandering; dreaming about becoming a professional footballer. Especially during maths lessons. Maths was the subject I hated the most. I spent much more time secretly working out how the league tables might look after the following Saturday's matches than trying to unravel the mysteries in the text book in front of me. Mind you, school must have somehow succeeded in getting the basics of arithmetic through to me because I have never had any problems working out league tables and goal averages!

I can vividly recollect being asked by Miss Copley, my teacher at Burnley Road School in Mytholmroyd, when I was seven or eight, what I wanted to be when I left school. Without hesitation I replied that I was going to be a professional footballer. "Don't be silly, Eric," replied Miss Copley. "You have to think of something that it is possible for you to do."

Miss Copley had heard it all before of course - becoming a footballer was every boy's dream. But she did not realise how determined this particular lad was to make his dream come true.

My day started with a paper round and I always had a tennis ball with me which I kicked against every wall that I passed. Every day I would get this little bit of early morning practice at ball-control but Thursday and Friday mornings were the problem days. Those were the days when the Radio Times and Woman's Own arrived at the paper shop. My newsbag weighed a ton and as I lugged it round it was difficult to carry it and kick the ball at the same time.

After the paper round it was off to school, kicking my tennis ball and every tin can that was unfortunate enough to get in the way. Then it was straight into the playground where I would join my mates for a game which could be anything from six a side to 20 a side. You know the type of game - with every kid determined to get as many touches as possible and chasing the ball like mad. Not too much in the way of tactics there! But we loved it.

I say we chased the ball - well "ball" is a bit of a euphemism. Sometimes we got lucky and would have an old case ball that someone had stolen from somewhere but more often it was a battered old tennis ball or a beach ball. Occasionally, one of the lads would nick a brand new ball from Woolworths (it could have been me but I can't remember!) but mostly we played with any old thing. Whatever the ragged circumstances, in each of our mind's eyes we were starring at some First Division ground or other. The games continued at break times, lunch times and after school. It was a shame those lessons used to get in the way!

School holidays were magic. Football every day - even in the middle of summer. It was either practicing or those wonderful 20-a-side games. I loved heading and I did most of my practicing under a railway arch. My pal crossed the ball for me to head a goal into the archway. I never missed - though, to be fair, the arch was about 40 feet high!

Another way I liked to practice was kicking a ball up our stairs at home and controlling it when it came down at all different angles.

It was an unusual sort of learning process but it didn't half help my control. The snag was, of course, for my parents who had to put up with a constant 'thump, thump, thump' from out in the hall. How many mothers would allow their lads to do that these days? My mum was a real gem.

Between the ages of six and 16, me and all my mates practiced and practiced and practiced - I reckon about ten times as much as youngsters today. I am certain that if we had received any sort of serious coaching we would have been better than today's kids but coaching hardly existed in those days. Practice will always make you better but a youngster needs advice too.

A good teacher is worth his or her weight in gold - nobody disputes that. Yet it has taken until only very recently, and in some cases is still not the case, for a football coach to be classed anywhere near as important as a teacher. They are in exactly the same business though - the business of helping young people make the most of their ability.

As a boy I was denied any coaching so I tried to learn what good habits were all about by watching matches whenever I could. I supported three clubs. First came Halifax Town, who were my local team because Halifax is only eight miles away from Hebden Bridge. The other two were Burnley and Manchester United, in that order.

Burnley, just over the Yorkshire/Lancashire border, were my nearest First Division club. They were a really big club in those days - and I hope they soon will be again - and I had a special affinity for them because even by the tender age of 14 I had "performed" at their ground, Turf Moor. I used to make the short trip over the Pennines with the Hebden Bridge Brass Band which played at Turf Moor on match-days. My job was to help carry the band's blanket round the edge of the pitch to collect coins thrown by the crowd. It was a real thrill to be able to walk round the touch-line at a big, and usually full, Football League ground. It was a bonus getting in for free too because if I hadn't been with the band I would certainly have

7

paid to stand on the terraces. As if that wasn't enough, it also enabled me to see such talented players as Jimmy Adamson and Jimmy McIlroy, the former Northern Ireland international, at close range for nothing.

I always rooted for Halifax and Burnley and looked for their results first. Then there was Manchester United. My father was a Lancashire man, born and bred in Manchester, and a United fan from his cradle. Naturally, I supported the same team as my dad.

As I passed through school, my ambition to play the great game professionally only burned brighter. To play for Burnley or United was my wildest dream but just to make a day-to-day living doing what I loved was my goal. I started local.

When I left Calder High School I achieved the first part of my ambition straight away. Halifax Town had monitored my progress playing for my school and district and offered me my first professional contract. When I scribbled my name on the forms in manager Willie Watson's tiny office I thought back to all those hours and hours of practice in the playground and the street and at the foot of the stairs and thought they had been well and truly worthwhile. I was a professional footballer. When I left Willie Watson's office having done the deed I was floating on air.

It meant so much to me and to this day I detest any footballer who does not give 100 per cent effort 100 per cent of the time in training and games. Professional footballers are a very priviliged breed. They should get down on their hands and knees and thank God that they are so lucky. It angers me to hear the way some of them moan and groan. Some of the foreigners, for example, come over here and are quite happy to accept lucrative wages but are then quick to complain. They moan about the skill level of our players, the food, the weather and the referees. It goes on and on - can you imagine the reaction in Italy if an English player complained about the food over there?

The last thing I am is a xenophobe. As you will read in a later

8

chapter I have the deepest admiration for, and have learned a great deal from, some of the foreign players who have come into the English game. But there are others who seeem to take a lot for granted. I mean, no-one puts a gun to their heads and forces them to come and play in this country do they?

Signing professional forms was the best moment of my life so far. It was the vital first step but secretly I already hoped that there were plenty more to come. I made my first-team debut for Halifax while still in my teens which was a little bit unusual at that time. I was surrounded by older and, sometimes, wiser players, one or two of whom - captain Alex South for example - helped me tremendously. Others, though, were a bit suspicious and sceptical about youngsters coming through quickly.

As I have mentioned, in the 1960s, players were not coached at all. Physical fitness was the order of the day. There were no tracksuit managers and no coaches and there was a huge anomaly in the training routines. All week on the training field, we would practice passing and playing football the right way then come match-day the manager's instructions completely ruined the week's training. He would say: "Don't take risks in your own half of the field", "Don't play too many sqaure passes", "Hit long balls to the strikers if you're in doubt". Before you went on to the field you were a nervous wreck. Negative thoughts took over. The illogicality of this soon struck me and has stuck with me ever since.

The Halifax players sometimes gave me advice but it wasn't always helpful. One piece I ended up not appreciating came before we played at Bradford Park Avenue, sadly no longer a Football League club. It was a big local derby with almost 20,000 spectators in the ground. At ten to three, a couple of our players came over and warned me about Jimmy Scoular.

Scoular, Bradford's player-manager, was a colossus. A talented former Scotland international wing-half, he had been to the top of the tree as a player. In 1955, he had skippered Newcastle United to

The View From the Dugout

their 3-1 FA Cup final win over Manchester City at Wembley, earning the man-of-the-match accolade that day for snuffing out the threat of City's up-and-coming centre-forward Don Revie. He was a tough guy. Putting it politely, he didn't take any prisoners.

Even approaching the end of his playing career, Scoular was a frightening looking man with legs like tree trunks. This young lad Harrison, this callow teenager, would be up against the mighty Scot so my team-mates advised me: "He is a tough guy so get your boot up high when you are tackling him."

Still wet behind the ears, I didn't really have much of a clue what they were talking about but I took their advice on board. Early in the game, the ball broke between Scoular and myself. It was a difficult bouncing ball and, as advised, I got my boot up high and, as the pros say, went right over the top. My right boot crashed into those tree-trunk thighs. He went down under the terrific impact and I thought good, he'll be carried off, and I won't have him to worry about any more. Unfortunately, he quickly got onto one knee, fixed me with a stare and shouted: "You're dead, son."

I was petrified. For the remaining 80 minutes of the match Scoular was intent on breaking me in half. It was like being chased round for more than an hour by an angry bull but somehow I survived. I went on to survive nearly 600 league and cup games and I did so with the assistance of valuable lessons like the one I learned that day: "Not all advice is good advice."

Jimmy Scoular was tough, and there were some very hard men about in those days, but without doubt the hardest man I ever played with or against was George Curtis, the Coventry City centre-half.

I played against him for Halifax Town, and unfortunately for me I had to play centre forward against him because we had all our strikers out injured. We played at Highfield Road, Coventry City's ground, and I hardly got a kick. Well, I'm telling a lie really because I got plenty of kicks - but they were all from George! I also played with him when we were doing our national service, and boy was I pleased to play with him rather than against him.

In those days you could get away with murder on the field and George really amused me when he answered a question of mine. He was five foot eleven, which is not very tall for a centre-half (centre-back in today's terms), and I asked him how he managed against six foot four centre-forwards (strikers in today's terms). He said: "No problem, because early in the game, when the first high ball comes up the middle, I head the back of the centre-forward's head - and he doesn't usually come back for more."

In the early days of my career I never suffered with nerves before or during games. As the years went by I did start getting nervous which was unusual - usually it is the other way round. One thing stayed constant, however. On the pitch, I always had an incredibly bad temper. Even as a teenager I wanted to win at all costs. It was such a matter of life and death to me that I would probably have kicked my grandmother up in the air if she had lined up in a team against me.

Even as a youngster making my way as a player at Halifax I had caught the coaching bug. I became qualified as soon as I could, lifting the number of qualified coaches at the Shay to the lofty figure of two - Alex South and myself. It was great for me because, still in my early days as a pro, I was already gaining experience coaching in the schools and local youth clubs. Even then I loved watching young players and helping them to improve. I leapt at every opportunity to put my coaching theory into practice and this was groundwork which was to prove priceless when I graduated to full-time coaching.

At one of the youth clubs in Halifax, I came across a real gem. He was only 12 but I could tell straight away he was special. I told him that with luck - and that vital ingredient of hard work - he would become a professional footballer and maybe even an international. I can usually appraise a young footballer in the pre-match warm-up session, especially their skills on the ball which this lad had by the bucketload. I look for balance, poise and the way they kick the ball.

The View From the Dugout

A good footballer can caress the ball at 70 miles an hour. This boy had tremendous skill and confidence, a wonderful touch and a good shot. His name was Frank Worthington.

The lad who I used to chide and encourage on to better things went on to play more league and cup games, and with bigger and better clubs, than I did. He played for England too, of course - and should have done a lot more often.

Frank still lives near me and I often play golf with him. He is a better golfer than me as well, showing excellent co-ordination with the smaller ball. He's a natural sportsman. Frank was a great footballer and what an entertainer. His goal for Bolton against Ipswich - that magical overhead dink over the defender followed by an unstoppable shot - is one of the truly great goals of all time. It will remain in the football archives forever.

I absolutely loved the life of a professional footballer; training all week then playing on Saturday. What a great life, and what characters you meet. One of the greatest characters I've met in football was our trainer at Halifax Town, a man called Harry Hubbick. Harry had been a famous player with Bolton Wanderers, who were in the first division of the Football League when Harry played for them.

He used to have the players in stitches every day. I was in the treatment room one Friday having my ankle strapped up by Harry. All of a sudden he got up and went to check the corridor. He then came back and proceeded to complain to me that the manager had picked the wrong side for the following day's game. Moments later in walked the manager to check on my ankle. He asked Harry how he thought we'd do in game. "No problem," said Harry, "We'll beat that lot tomorrow, especially with that team."

On another occasion all the players, who used to wind him up something rotten, asked him to the judge in a kangaroo court against one of the young players, Tony Field, who eventually went on to play with Pele at New York Cosmos and who had been sent off in the previous weekend's game. We told Harry to never mind about the

12

F.A. ban, he was to sentence him and he had the choice of banning him for 21 days or three weeks. After a minute's deliberation Harry said that we were to throw the book at him and ban him for 21 days!

Perhaps the best Harry Hubbick story though was when he was returning from training at a local park with Bob Worthington, brother of Frank, in his car along with assorted balls and flag poles. Harry was chatting away with Bob and driving at a snail's pace as he drove up to the Shay. The driver behind decided to overtake just as Harry turned right into the Shay without signalling. The two cars collided and the other driver got out fully expecting Harry to admit responsibility for the accident through not signalling, but Harry was having none of it. "Couldn't you see that I've got my Halifax Town tracksuit on and I was obviously turning into the Shay!" he screamed. What a character. Believe you me, there are no Harry Hubbick's in football these days.

For 10 years I did the business at Halifax as a defensive midfielder - wing-half as it was called then. I was an effective player - a stopper, I suppose you might say, but I have often wondered how much better I might have been with some proper advice. Without such advice I was left to fall back on what I was born with: a tough tackle, a sense of organisation and a desire to win. I was a bit of a monster on the pitch and, unfortunately, temper and technique have got to be prefectly balanced with each other to make a happy mix. When you lose your temper, as I frequently did (heaven knows what referees would have made of me these days), your skill level drops. Your control and passing deteriorates and you are of far less value to your team.

I will always maintain that if only a manager or coach had sat me down and given me better advice, and maybe one of two well-timed bollockings, I would have been a far better player but in my 17 years as a pro not one of them told me to cool it. For me to carry on trying to break opponents in half was obviously part of their game plan. That was life in the lower divisions.

The View From the Dugout

After 10 years of harassing opposing strikers on behalf of Halifax I went to see the manager about my benefit money. In those days, ten years service with a club was supposed to be rewarded by a £750 one-off payment, a sort of loyalty bonus. This, I felt, I had fully earned. Players were arriving at the Shay from other clubs and receiving signing-on fees and I knew that, as a local lad, I loved the club more than they did. I was well within my rights to ask for the money.

The manager soon came back to me with a sheepish expression on his face. He said the directors couldn't afford to pay my benefit money. I was furious. I had committed myself totally to the club for 10 years and was now asking only for what was due to me. It was not as though I was trying to get something extra. I was angry and hurt that they could turn round and treat a loyal player in that way. Feeling totally taken for granted, I asked for a transfer and decided that whichever club came in for me and offered a £750 signing on fee, I would join.

A few days later Hartlepool United made me an offer (I thought about holding out for Burnley or Manchester United but it could have been a long wait!). Hartlepools agreed to pay me the signing on fee and I said to Shirley, my wife: "Get your bags packed. We're off."

I drove us the 100 miles or so up to our club house and that first car-ride up to the north-east coast was a real ordeal. Shirley was pregnant with our first daughter and cried all the way. I had uprooted her not to go to Old Trafford or Anfield or St James' Park - but Victoria Park! When she saw the ground I think she felt like bursting into tears all over again. Halifax's dear old Shay Ground was ramshackle but Victoria Park made the Shay look like the Maracana. All the paint was peeling and the creaking stands looked like they would blow over in a stiff breeze. Spectators used to wipe their feet on the way out.

The stadium was decrepit, the supporters were few and far between, the team was near the bottom of the Fourth Division and a bitterly cold wind seemed to be blowing constantly in off the North Sea. "It's the right move," I promised Shirley, with fingers, toes and just about everything else I could possibly cross crossed.

I could never have dreamed just how right it was. Because if I hadn't joined Hartlepool I wouldn't have been among the priviliged few to witness the birth of a managerial legend. A man from whom I was to learn a vast amount.

Not long after I landed at Hartlepools United arrived the man who, in a few short months, was to mould much of my coaching philosophy for life. Enter the Boss. Brian Clough.

3.

Life with Brian

BRIAN CLOUGH ARRIVED AT HARTLEPOOLS like John Wayne bursting through the doors of a wild-west saloon.

Nobody knew at the time, of course, that here was one of the all-time great managers taking his first steps in the business. It was just a case, as far as anybody was aware, of another ex-footballer having a stab at management, if a little earlier than usual because his playing career had been cut short by injury. Nothing too controversial was expected. A nervous young manager who wouldn't say boo to a goose? Not exactly. It didn't take long for the new man to start raising eyebrows and bruising egos.

The particular saloon into which Clough, with his sidekick Peter Taylor, had landed was one of the least salubrious around. At Victoria Park, when we turned up for training it was a case of first in, best dressed. Our training kit was not the best - and that's being kind. The players just picked their kit up from the boiler room where it had been left to dry from the previous day. Well, we didn't actually pick it up - we just whistled for it and it walked across the room to us!

Hartlepools United was run by Ernie Ord, a man who contolled it from top to bottom. He liked to be in charge of everyone and in contol of everything but soon found out that Clough was a young man who didn't kow-tow to anyone.

Ernie Ord owned the club and ruled the roost and I think when he appointed Brian and Peter he thought he was getting a pair of rookies who would just be grateful for their chance to get into Football League management. Somebody he could control. Control Cloughie ? It would be easier to control the wind.

Blunt, aggressive, volatile, arrogant and downright rude. Cloughie, even as one of the youngest League managers ever, was them all. But he earned respect. He was also capable of great kindness, compassion and warmth but, most importantly, he was a unique coach who immediately revealed an ability to make half-decent players into good ones. Later on, of course, he showed he could turn good players into great ones.

Clough's organisational skills were very simple. He told every player in the team their role and demanded that each carried out his role. There were no ifs, buts or maybes. You did it or you were out of the team and if you were difficult you were out of the club. I have seen Cloughie crucify people. He ruled with a rod of iron but he was focussed on one thing. Success.

I did not escape his savagery. He told me that I had a big mouth because I was always having a go at referees. Next time I argued with a ref, he said, he would fine me. The next time came very quickly. I mouthed off to the referee, got booked - there were no yellow and red cards back in the 1960s - and sure enough Brian hit me with a heavy fine. He knew that a lot of players were hurt more by a blow to the pay-packet than any punishment they took on the field. His action cured my verbosity. I never argued with referees again because I would have to go home with a half-empty pay packet. I would get a rollicking from Mr Clough and then another one from Mrs Shirley Harrison because our weekly income dropped appreciably.

My next-door neighbour and playing colleague, Stan Storton,

17

also got on the wrong side of the Boss. He was fined a week's wages for arguing with Clough so he stormed into the manager's office to confront him. Stan started arguing again and came out looking as green as grass. His fine had been doubled to two weeks' wages! No player could argue with the Boss and win.

It was just as bad in the dressing room, that ultimate inner-sanctum of any team. Normally the dressing room is a refuge. A safe haven where players can have a right old moan about the manager. But Peter Taylor told all the players that if he heard any of the players moaning or generally having a go at the manager he would report the utterances straight back to him. We were snookered all over the place but it fostered uniformity among the players. When you are in the same boat you all have to row in the same direction if you are going to get anywhere.

The "them and us" mentality was reinforced by us always having to call the manager 'Boss.' I hesitate to call him Brian, even now. One of the players called him Brian and was immediately hit by a fine. You always had to call him Boss - just to remind you (and anyone else that might happen to be within earshot) that that's what he was.

Despite all the fines and the regular rollickings, I quickly realised that here was a manager from which I could learn much. His teaching was music to my ears because his words were preparing me for a long coaching career. His strength of character and self-belief made him a powerful motivator, but as well as a forceful personality he was also a coach of great intelligence and vision. I took everything he said on board and stored it for future use.

Every Monday morning we had a team meeting about the previous Saturday's game. I grew to enjoy these for two reasons. The first reason was that the Boss always liked a trier and I always worked hard for him and got stuck in. I got into trouble now and then for over-aggressive play but that meant I was never in much trouble with Clough. Aggression and passion were what he demanded from his players.

The second reason was my thirst for knowledge. Clough was a real stickler for homework and went through every opposing player with a fine-toothed comb, mentioning their good and bad points. He was red hot on the defensive side of the game and any player who turned his back on the ball, cowardly ducked out of a tackle, did not attempt to win a heading duel or found himself out of position through lack of concentration, was slaughtered. Players were more afraid of the dressing-down they would get for backing out than any injury they might collect getting stuck in.

But Clough's methods were not just about shouting and bullying. Sure, there was plenty of those but there was also a lot of careful, well thought-out strategy towards increasing the levels of organisation and team spirit. I was beginning to understand how to get a team to defend together as a unit.

I was also learning to spot the characteristics required to make a good professional footballer. It was ingrained in me at that very early stage that players are totally responsible for their own performances on the pitch. A manager can cajole and advise and rant and rave but once the players are over the white line it is up to them. Clough let us know that if we took responsibility on the pitch we were OK. If any player did not, and just played for himself, he was out of the team.

Clough's philosophy on offensive play was fascinating. He wanted quick, simple passing and put the emphasis on strikers being able to hold up the ball or turn with the ball. If a striker was not comfortable with the ball at his feet, he was no good to the manager. Clough had been a great centre-forward - who knows what he would have achieved if injury had not ended his career in 1960 after he had gained just two England caps? - so he knew what he was talking about.

He said something to one of our strikers that I had never heard from a manager before and I have not heard since. Ernie

19

The View From the Dugout

Phythian had just joined us from Bolton Wanderers and the Boss said to him: "You have got the number nine on your back. I pay you to score goals and if you don't, I'll sign a player who will."

Every other manager I have worked with has protected their strikers, telling them to keep getting into the right positions and the goals will come. "Don't worry about missing chances," is the usual, reassuring message. Confidence is a fragile commodity and managers sometimes have to pussy-foot around their players and often strikers more than any.

Not with Clough. Never. "Keep missing chances," he warned Ernie, "and you're out." It worked. Phythian scored goals and Hartlepools developed into the best side they had had in years.

Discovering and developing good strikers has always been a Clough trait. Under him at Derby County, Kevin Hector became an England international. At Nottingham Forest, Tony Woodcock, Gary Birtles and Peter Davenport all made the England team. Brian was also financially prudent and sold those three to make Forest a tasty profit.

Brian Clough is unique. Totally different to any other manager I ever worked with. Never, ever predictable. In the 1960s, playing on New Year's Day was not unusual but what happened on New Year's Eve 1965 certainly was. We were playing Tranmere Rovers at Prenton Park and stayed the night before the game at a hotel on the Wirral. All the players had finished their evening meal and were ready to drift off to our rooms and watch TV as usual when Brian asked us all what we wanted to drink. We all looked at each other in amazement because it was clear he was not just talking about orange juice.

Alcohol was normally totally out of the question on the night before a match but we all listened in amazement as Clough barked: "Come on, what do you want?" Most of the players ordered pints of lager, which were rapidly downed. When we had finished a pint apiece he ordered the same again. When the second pint had gone down Mr Clough told us all to get to bed. I don't know of any other manager who would have done that. Mind you, it wasn't one of the great man's more successful brainwaves. We lost.

Clough was a total one-off. In many ways he was the most thorough and diligent manager you could find yet all the time I worked under him I can never remember practicing corner kicks or free-kicks, either taking them or defending them. The players were left to organise themselves when the situations arose on the pitch. It would be totally alien to every other manager I have ever worked with - but that's Clough for you. I suppose he trusted himself to send out a team capable of sorting themselves out at set-pieces.

My only regret is that I did not stay longer with Brian Clough because I would have learned so much more about coaching but he arrived at the club at a time when I had already decided my career needed freshening up with a move.

Only a couple of days after he arrived at Hartlepool, Clough called the players together. He outlined his demand for 100 per cent commitment to the club at all times and told us in no uncertain terms that anyone who did not want to play for him should come and see him after training.

It was not that I did not want to play for the new manager but I was unsettled and wanted to leave. The only way to make any money in the lower divisions was to move from club to club and get signing-on fees. I went to see him and used the footballers' old favourite excuse: the wife could not settle in the area. It was a brief meeting and he said that he would bear that in mind.

True to his word, at the end of the season I was given a free transfer and was on my bike to Barrow. I had spent less than a season under Clough but in that time had become a much wiser footballer and what I learned was to form a solid foundation for the rest of my career.

Next time I had contact with Brian was in his office at Derby County at their old Baseball Ground. I was still playing for Barrow when Peter Taylor contacted me to say that the Boss wanted to interview me with a view to me taking over as youth coach at Derby. Naturally, I was very excited and rang a friend of mine, Willie Carlin, who played in midfield for Derby's first team and who had been a team-mate of mine at Halifax. I stayed the night with Willie and his family in Derby and on the morning of the interview, Willie drove me to the ground. As I got out of the car, he said; "You know what the Boss is like, so give as good as you get."

Peter Taylor met me and said I would have to wait because the Boss was showing the Lord Mayor around the ground. (I'm not quite sure who would call who 'sir' in that situation - but I think I can guess!) Eventually, he arrived and the first thing he said to me was typically blunt. "If someone had said when I was manager of Hartlepool and you were a player, that I would ever offer you a job on my coaching staff, I would have said they were mad." But after the usual bravado came the real reason for my visit. He asked me a few questions and said he would be very interested to hear the answer to his final question. "I know you are friendly with one of our players, Willie Carlin," he said. "Now if you were taking a training session with Willie and he was messing around could you give him a rollicking?" My answer was that of course I could. "The job's yours," said Clough.

He also wanted me to be reserve player/coach and I found the prospect very exciting but a disappointment waited round the corner. Barrow manager Norman Bodell refused to release me from my playing contract. Clough, evidently very keen to get me, then said I could become a full-time member of his coaching staff, never mind that I wouldn't be able to play, but I turned the job down because I wanted to carry on playing.

I have always wondered what would have been in store for me as one of Brian Clough's coaches. The way things have worked out I could not possibly have asked for more satisfaction and pleasure from my career but, if things had been different, Barrow's mean-spirited approach might have cost me dear.

I still find myself wanting to refer to Brian as Mr Clough as I keep thinking that, when he reads this book, he will send me a fine in the post if I call him Brian. I can't praise him, as a coach or man-manager, highly enough. It is scandalous that he was not appointed England manager at the height of his career but anyone who knows football knows why. Brian Clough, a truly great manager, was too outspoken. He would have rocked the FA boat, upset the starched-shirts and often done the exact opposite of what the establishment wanted him to do.

He might just have won us the World Cup too though.

4.

Bill Shankly and Everton

I SPENT THREE SEASONS WITH BARROW then two down the coast at Southport before going back to Barrow for another season at Holker Street. Both those clubs were in the Football League when I played for them and it's very sad to see them languishing below the League now. I seem to have left a jinx at all my clubs - the last club I played for was Scarborough, who have unfortunately gone the same way although hopefully they will one day return to the Football League, like my first club Halifax.

Whichever club I played for, I threw myself fully into coaching; in schools, youth clubs, universities and also for the Football Association. I obtained my full coaching qualifications, and became increasingly keen to get into coaching full-time at a league club. I absolutely loved it - dealing with youngsters and helping them make the most of their talent. I still do.

My lucky break came through one of my fellow coaches at the Football Association. Ray Minshull, the FA's head of coaching in the north-west, was also youth development officer at Everton. He rang me to say that there was a vacancy for a youth coach at Goodison

Park and he would like me to go for an interview. I jumped at the chance.

Harry Catterick, that great Everton manager, met me in reception and ushered me into his office. If my interview with Brian Clough at Derby was a little strange, this was much more orthodox, just like a well-organised interview should proceed. After many searching questions Catterick finally offered me the job and I accepted it without hesitation.

The interview had a real twist in the tail. Catterick told me that I would be in charge of 16 apprentices, between the ages of 16 and 19, and some of them could be very difficult. If I was soft with them, he said, they would get the upper hand and if that happened I'd be out. No questions asked. Sacked. Talk about laying it on the line!

He never had to sack me. And believe me, dealing with those "difficult" lads can be the most satisfying and rewarding of all. They are the ones most likely to waste their ability and to prevent them squandering that rare God-given talent is a real thrill.

There was one other matter to resolve before I could join Everton. I had, of course, missed out on the chance to join Derby County because Barrow wouldn't release me from my contract. When the chance to go to Everton came up I was playing for Scarborough so was a little anxious in case a similar situation occurred. I need not have worried. Their attitude was in a totally different class to the one Barrow had showed.

Under the management of Colin Appleton, Scarborough were doing well at the time. They were on a good run in the FA Trophy and, with the possibility of a Wembley final in their sights, naturally their directors did not want to let me go. Colin, though, realised that it was a great opportunity for me and persuaded his board to release me. That was a gesture typical of a fine man who was also a seriously under-rated manager. I had played under Colin at Barrow where, on ever-meagre resources, he nearly got the club promoted to the old Division Two. We had some superb experienced professionals - Fred

The View From the Dugout

Else, Ron McGarry and Howard Riley - in the team but it was Colin who held it all together. Not only was he a fine manager but he could kick a football further in a carpet slipper with his left foot than many players could with boots on!

He went on to manage Scarborough to three FA Trophy final victories and then did an excellent job reviving Hull City before replacing John Toshack at Swansea City. Unfortunately, finances were not available there and he could not kick-start the Vetch Field outfit but I have the greatest respect for Colin and I was delighted when he agreed to do some scouting for me at Manchester United. I am amazed that his managerial ability was never recognised at the top level.

So, with the assistance of Colin's input, I had got my chance at a First Division club. Everton is a great football club with a wonderful set of supporters and I loved every minute of the nine years I was to spend there. Now I was serving my real coaching apprenticeship. Even though I had been involved in coaching for 17 years previously, here I was dealing with high quality players. It was a big step up and a real challenge - and I was helped to meet it by another man whose place in the football pantheon is, like Clough's, secure forever.

As I settled in at Goodison, I was privileged to get to know the legendary Bill Shankly. He had retired as manager of Liverpool but still lived in a house overlooking Everton's Bellefield training ground so used to call in most days to have a cup of tea and a chat. As soon as I knew Bill was at the training ground, I would drop what I was doing and hunt him out. We talked at length with me hanging on his every word.

He was a football fanatic and you could understand his great powers of motivating players just by talking to him. I was fantastically lucky to have the opportunity to learn from such a great tutor. Getting the chance to talk to Bill on a one-to-one basis was like winning the lottery.

The brilliance of Bill's advice was often in its simplicity. Here's a classic example. He told me to get the groundsman to mark out eight white lines, about 25 yards long, on various parts of the training ground. Then get one player to stand at one end of a line and another player at the other. Give them a ball and tell them to pass it to each other along the white line. He said: "Get them to do it until they can all pass the ball straight down the line. If they can't pass the ball straight, they can't play football." So simple but so effective. It improved the players' skills, taught them the importance of doing the simple things correctly and gave the coach a good insight into which ones had the most natural ability. Generations of Liverpool players have been able to pass the ball well and that's down to Shanks.

I don't use the white-line method now but follow the same principal by getting players to pass between traffic cones. Gary Neville knows what I mean because I made him do it for hours at the Cliff and it worked for him. Not only did he reach the first team at United but went on to become a regular member of the England squad.

After working with the Everton youth team for four years, I became reserve-team coach, before stepping up to first-team coach under manager Gordon Lee. Everton was a good club to work for and always promoted internally if they believed that you could do the job. When they moved me up to work with the first team they clearly believed I could handle the job. So did I but in fact it was soon clear that I was still quite low on the learning curve.

I made a lot of mistakes when I first worked with the first team and only gradually came to realise that coaching had many facets to it. Observation, tactics, team coaching and individual coaching were all important areas and ones at which I felt I was fairly good. But then there was man-management. This I thought I knew all about but soon learned that it was a department in which I was very lacking.

My strong desire to win led to a very bad temper when things were going wrong on the field. This resulted in my bawling out some players and arguing too much which meant they did not always perform to the best of their ability. Some players just won't respond to a belligerent approach. There were times when I thought that I was right and they thought that they were right and too much friction developed. Being relatively young and lacking in diplomacy, everything I thought spilled out of me. I did not talk behind other players backs but, if I had something to say, I told them to their faces. In team meetings if I was criticising players I would name names. While that appears to be the right thing to do, believe me, sometimes it's not. Senior players - especially international ones - do not like being criticised. The players involved were furious that I had pointed a finger at them and I became disliked by a few of them. When a coach is opposed by a clique of players, especially if they are high-profile players, his authority is challenged, if not undermined. With hindsight I should have been more crafty like some coaches I could mention.

I had made mistakes - and when that happens there are two things you can do. Be stubborn and keep on making them or get something positive from the experience and learn. I learned. To be truthful I knew I had opened my big mouth too many times without thinking.

The fact that I learned that lesson was to prove a big help to Manchester United later on. I became more adept at dealling with players and when Brian Kidd was appointed United's assistant manager in 1991 I quickly advised him to stay cool and not fall out with first-team players. I realised that falling out with the first-team is a job for the manager.

At Everton, I developed a technique which I continued to use throughout my coaching career. It involved established first-team players, many of them internationals, who for one reason or another had to play in the reserves or junior teams. I first tried it out with Joe Royle, who is now manager of Manchester City.

Joe was a great centre forward and is a lovely person. On this occasion he had undergone surgery on a back injury and, well on his way back to full fitness, had to play for Everton's A team. It can be difficult for first-team players to perform amongst the kids at junior level but I have always expected any professional footballer to do their job properly whatever the circumstances.

With this in mind, much of my team talk revolved around Joe. I told all the young players that they were very lucky to be playing with a great player and England international. It was an excellent experience for them and, if they had any sense, they would learn from it. I was not trying to suck up to Joe - it was just a case of showing a senior player the respect he deserved. It worked because Joe, the model professional, worked hard and everybody got something out of the game.

I have always worked on the same principle when senior players had to play in the junior teams. One funny instance comes to mind from my time, later on, at Manchester United. Gordon Strachan, a wonderful skilful player and a really great character, once played for United's A team in similar circumstances to the ones I just described about Joe Royle. I worked on the usual principle, giving Gordon a big build-up before the game, telling all my young players that he would produce a brilliant performance and they would certainly learn a lot from him. I could not believe my eyes when Strach had a nightmare. The harder he tried, the worse it got for him and, with him being a really proud person and a fine pro, he was devastated after the game.

He apologised to me and all the young players and after he had showered he came upstairs to the staff-room for a cup of tea and asked me why he had played so badly. I saw the funny side of it and started to laugh but Strach was not in a laughing mood. I told him that sometimes you start a game badly and you just can't get going but he would not accept this and went home with his tail between his legs. He must have been really worried because two or three times the following week he apologised to me for his performance. Whatever the circumstances, whether it was an FA Cup final or a Lancashire League game, Gordon Strachan always wanted to play well. That is to his great credit.

I had only been working at Everton a few weeks when Harry Cooke, the chief scout, asked me to go and watch Manchester United as Everton were due to play them shortly. I had to write out a match report and, with it being my first, I found it quite difficult. It was certainly not as daunting as what followed though.

A scouting report is very important to managers as it goes into a lot of detail on how the opposition plays. I was very careful to write every possible detail on United and I presented the report to Harry Catterick, hoping it met with his approval. A big shock was waiting for me on the Friday morning before the Manchester United game. The manager always had his team-talk on the Friday and, to my astonishment, I was summoned to the team meeting. With the players all assembled there, quite out of the blue, Catterick then said, I have read your report, now I want you to talk to the team and tell them how Manchester United play. I was virtually giving the team talk! I did not have chance to be nervous. I just walked in and started speaking. The manager never said whether the report was good or bad, or my speech was good or bad. Talk about being thrown in at the deep end!

The manager was testing me and another test soon arrived. I was taking a training session when Catterick appeared from nowhere. He stood alongside me and grilled me about every facet of my session. I came through with flying colours because all through my coaching career, I have planned and wrote down all my training and coaching sessions so I was never found wanting in my organisation.

At lunchtime that day, I told the rest of the coaching staff what had happened. I asked them what would have happened if I had conducted a poor, disorganised coaching session and they said the manager would probably have sacked me - or certainly given me a right rollicking. It was in-at-the-deep-end stuff but a great apprenticeship and just what I needed. It made me understand that I was at the top level now and dealing with top players and coaches. At that level, it's sink or swim and those who are sinking will not find too many people interested in throwing out lifebelts.

Unfortunately in 1981 I left Everton under a cloud. The chairman, Sir Philip Carter, as he is now, called me into his office and told me he had sacked the manager, Gordon Lee. He seemed genuinely upset but then told me that the board wanted me to stay on because they thought I had done very well in my time with the club. He also said that the club had no idea who the new manager would be.

I found that hard to believe - what sort of a First Division club sacks a manager without having planned for the future? What they obviously did not know was whether the new manager would bring his own assistant with him.

I was reasonably relaxed, as far as my personal job security was concerned, after that chat but still felt extremely upset for Gordon who is a good, genuine man. We have kept in touch over the years.

With indecent haste, Howard Kendall, who had been manager at Blackburn Rovers, was installed at Goodison. I had been right not to believe the chairman. Howard quickly spoke to me and said that he was bringing his assistant Mick Heaton to the club. Immediately I told Howard that I was on my bike. Howard told me not to be so hasty and to have a think about the situation but I could not get away quickly enough. After my departure my suspicions that the club had been less than straight with me were confirmed. Everton went on a Far Eastern tour to Japan and it transpired that Kendall had been given his club blazer before even arriving at Goodison Park. He had been measured for it whilst he was still at Blackburn. This proved in my mind that I had made the correct decision to leave the Merseyside club.

I had some wonderful years at Everton. It is a great club, with good directors and loyal supporters and I still look for their result.

The View From the Dugout

The saddest thing was to leave behind all the talented youngsters I had brought into the club. Lads who would mature into full internationals like right-back Gary Stevens who went on to win 46 caps for England. Ironically, Gary had lived opposite me when I played for Barrow and I often saw him playing and practicing in his garden. Gary was a very pleasant lad and a quick learner with pace and excellent positional skills. Rangers bought him from Everton which made the club a vast profit before, sadly, injury brought a premature end to his career at Tranmere Rovers. However, being a bright young man he studied hard and qualified as a physiotherapist. A valuable lesson there for all youngsters: get yourselves educated. A footballer's working life is a short one.

Another chapter of my working life had closed. Leaving a club of Everton's stature is not something you do lightly but I had to look forward. Everton is a big club and there were not too many places you could move up to from there. Not many clubs are bigger. Luckily I found one. The biggest.

5.

Snapped up by Big Ron

I WAS DELIGHTED AND VERY PROUD to read in Ron Atkinson's autobiography that Ron believes that I was one of the best signings that he ever made for Manchester United. When he added that all the young players who have come through the ranks at United owe a lot to my patience, kindness and ability, a certain Mrs Harrison started to wonder if they were talking about the man she married!

Ron Atkinson was always very supportive to me. Ron is a great bloke with bags of confidence, a superb personality and a wonderful sense of humour. I loved every minute of my time with him. He made a lot of changes to the coaching staff at Old Trafford, bringing in Mick Brown as his assistant and Brian Whitehouse as his reserve team manager. Tony Collins came in as chief scout and Jimmy Hedridge as physiotherapist so it was a real time of transition at the club.

Jimmy, who was a lovely guy, tragically died of a heart attack in 1982. Everyone at the club, especially Ron, Mick and the first team players who witnessed his death, were stunned and devastated. Jimmy died on the training ground doing the job he did so brilliantly, looking after the welfare of the players. Shortly after we so cruelly lost him, another Jimmy took over as physiotherapist. Jimmy McGregor arrived from Everton, my former club, so I was reunited with another good friend but the tragedy of Jimmy Hedridge's death stayed with us all for a long time.

Ron Atkinson not only made changes to the backroom staff, he quickly made changes to the playing ranks. Always adventurous and blessed with the courage of his own convictions, he brought in John Gidman, Frank Stapleton, Bryan Robson, Remi Moses, Arnold Muhren, Gordon Strachan, Alan Brazil, Jesper Olsen, Peter Barnes, Colin Gibson, Terry Gibson, Chris Turner, John Siveabeck, Peter Davenport and, on loan, Laurie Cunningham and Gareth Crooks.

Ron had been fourth choice - behind Lawrie McMenemy, Bobby Robson and Ron Saunders - to replace Dave Sexton as United manager but if that suggests one or two of United's directors had their doubts about him, there was no lack of confidence from the man himself. Whatever the job that Ron took on, whatever the challenge he faced, he never, ever contemplated failure. He had come up the hard way as a player with Oxford United and a manager with Kettering Town and Cambridge United before really making a name for himself at the Hawthorns. He lifted West Bromwich Albion to third spot in the First Division, which earned them a UEFA Cup place, all the while building a reputation for playing attractive football. "Too many people in football are too serious," he said after settling into the Old Trafford hot seat. "I want my team to excite, to be positive and to have flair."

There was though, behind the grin and the wisecracks, a deadly serious desire to succeed. Ron has a reputation as a bit flash with the champagne and the jewellery and cigars and certainly he has a flamboyant streak but I can tell you he is also a thorough professional. He devoted so much of his time to the club and not just the first team. He loved watching the youngsters play. All in all he was a very good manager. Under him, the first team always tried to play open, attacking football and I was deeply saddened when he got the sack. He had done a great job, guiding United to lift the FA Cup in 1983 and 1985 against Brighton and Everton. Perhaps with a little more time he could have brought the League Championship to Old Trafford.

For me personally, a move to Manchester United meant I really had a chance to start building a long-term youth structure based upon all that I had learned in the hours and hours listening to the likes of Brian Clough and Bill Shankly. I was also determined to avoid the mistakes I had seen other coaches make.

I vowed when I joined United that I would always encourage young players to play properly. I have always wondered if I could have achieved more as a player given the right coaching and encouragement as an apprentice so I decided that all the youngsters that would ever look to me for help would be given it. They would also be brought up with the right principles. I hope that no boy that ever passed under my supervision could ever look back and say: "I didn't get a fair crack of the whip."

At United, from Monday to Friday, we played seven-a-sides or had practice matches in which all the players passed the ball on the floor and played in a nice relaxed manner. One of Manchester United's great strengths in coaching is that the manager, coaches and youth coaches all use the same basic principles. These revolve around a tried and tested formula which is made clear to all coaches when they join the club. This consistency of approach means all the teams play the same way and players become accustomed to ideas from which they never deviate, irrespective of the level at which they are representing the club. That makes it so much easier to move from one team to another at Old Trafford.

When I was youth coach at Everton, I always thought that the young players at Manchester United were a bit soft. I felt that if we got stuck into them they would fold and usually we could beat them quite comfortably.

The View From the Dugout

This fact was on my mind when I joined United and I soon found out that my impressions of some of the young players at United were correct. Our A team played away at Bolton Wanderers very early in my first season. The events at Bolton that day convinced me I was right.

When I worked with young players at Everton and we were playing at Manchester United I always told my lads to get stuck in and ruffle a few feathers. I genuinely believed that United's players were soft. It usually worked because we did not have too many problems beating them.

One of my first games in charge of United's youth team was at Bolton which we played at 11am on a midweek day which was a bit unusual. I vividly remember a lot of the Bolton first-team players coming down to watch the second half of the game and I was squirming with embarrassment on the toouchline at our pathetic display. We were gutless and got hammered 5-0. The Bolton youngsters were delighted and the watching Bolton first team lapped up every minute of seeing their juniors wipe the floor with United's boys.

After the game I gave our young players the rocket of their lives. What I had seen had hurt me as their coach and I knew they should have been hurting too. I told them they would never produce a performance like that again - in fact, I said that was the last time that a Manchester United youth team would ever surrrender. I then did something I had never done before and have not done since. I told the players to get staight back on the bus without getting showered or changed and we went straight back to the Cliff training ground. In silence they travelled the short journey back to our base and then I told them we were going straight out to train. We did very little actually but it was an effective way of letting them know that what they had produced was totally unacceptable.

Actually, the surprise training session nearly backfired on me because sitting in his office upstairs was Ron Atkinson. He called me up when the boys finally finished and demanded to know what I was playing at. He certainly wasn't pleased. When I explained my reasons he just about accepted it but it just proved that when players let themselves down and don't take responsibility on the pitch they let everyone down. Ron was hurt. He knew that his club would be judged by what everyone present at that game at Bolton had seen.

To be fair to the youngsters involved, the message got through very quickly because a performance like that was not repeated. We never surrendered again.

In that youth squad that I inherited in 1981 were two great strikers who would never surrender to anybody. I knew instantly that Mark Hughes and Norman Whiteside would both play at the highest level in the game.

But for a bad knee injury when he was 16, Belfast-born Norman would have been world class. I am totally convinced of that. He had everything apart from pace and I am sure that if he had not been dogged by that bad knee, he would have been quick too.

I have rarely seen a young player have such an instinct for making the right choices on a football field. During the hurly-burly of a game players have to make many split-second decisions. This is where a football-brain is important and Norman's was as agile as any player I've known at that age.

He was handling top-flight football when most boys are still at school. At 17, Norman became the youngest player ever to appear in a World Cup finals when he pulled on the famous green shirt of Northern Ireland. Even before then he had already scored on his full debut for Manchester United in a 2-0 win at home to Stoke City on the last day of the season. Within little more than a year, he was to become the youngest player to score in a Wembley final (against Liverpool in the Milk Cup) and then the youngest to net in an FA Cup final (a header against Brighton).

A coach only had to tell Norman something once and it stuck. He had a great brain to go with his courage, strength and technique. He could look after himself on the field too. In fact, he was a bit nasty at times but I didn't mind that. A lot of the great strikers (only later did Norman drop back into midfield) had to have a nasty streak because strikers then didn't receive the same amount of protection from referees that they do today. They got kicked a lot and, with the tackle from behind still permissible, defenders took liberties.

I'm not surprised that since being forced by injury into retirement at the cruelly early age of 25, Norman Whiteside has applied himself well to another career. He has become a podiatrist for the PFA and has obviously used his intelligence to pursue an alternative career which is still linked with football.

Mark Hughes is an odd mixture. Very quiet off the field and a lion - or should I say a dragon in his case - on it. He was similar to Whiteside in many ways - aggressive, strong, brave and skilful. Hughes is still playing and will go down in history as one of the truly great players.

The match that saw Mark really arrive, in my opinion, came in April 1984, a European Cup Winners Cup semi-final second leg against Juventus in Turin. Juventus had earned a 1-1 draw in the first leg at Old Trafford and boasted a star-studded team which included Zoff, Platini, Cabrini, Boniek, Rossi, Tardelli and one of the toughest defenders in Italian football, Gentili.

Well, Gentili marked Sparky Hughes that night. He marked him alright - on his ankles, calves and knees. Almost every part of Sparky's body below the waist was marked. Hughsie kept getting knocked down and kept getting back up and, for a young lad, which he was then, he showed amazing courage especially against a colossus like Gentili.

After 75 minutes Hughsie had had enough and he went straight through Gentili catching him with a brutal tackle which, in truth, the defender had coming to him. Gentili went down as if he had been hit by a bus, as a lot of the foreigners do, but to be fair to him he got quickly up. I feared for Mark but Gentili did not clatter Hughsie again - he had obviously got the message.

Eric "Chopper" Harrison, aged 18 months

Halifax Town - August 1959

Back Row: Stan Lonsdale, Frank Large, Phil Roscoe, Arthur Johnson, Roy Lorenson, Eric Harrison

Front Row: Doug Fletcher, Conway Smith, Peter Tilley, Andy McCall, Alan Blackburn

The one and only Brian Clough
I learnt a lot from Brian when I played under him at Hartlepool,
his first managerial appointment.

Barrow vs. Southampton, F.A. Cup 3rd Round 1966

That's me heading the ball with Martin Chivers, a future England
international, looking on and Fred Else in goal

Barrow A.F.C. in 1967/8, the season we won promotion to the Third Division.

That's me third from the left on the second row from the back.

Harry Catterick and Colin Harvey
Harry was a legend on Merseyside as the manager at Everton and
gave me my first coaching job. Colin began his coaching career
while I was at Everton and he eventually had a spell as Manager.

A gathering of top F.A. coaches at Lilleshall in the mid-1960's.
I'm not that easy to spot but perhaps you can see Jimmy Hill, Malcolm Allison and Jack Charlton amongst others.

The Great Bill Shankly

We lost 2-1, though I thought we were unlucky, and the scene in the dressing room was one of doom and gloom. Ron Atkinson told the players that they had performed very well and had nothing to be ashamed of. About 20 minutes after the final whistle, Ron and I went out of the dressing room and, with no invitation to go into the opposing manager's room, we just stood in the corridor talking about the game. Suddenly Gentili, immaculately dressed, came marching up to us and I thought: "Here's trouble." How wrong you can be. He proceeded to tell us that our number ten, the young boy, would become a top player. It was music to my ears and praise indeed from a defender who had marked some of the world's best forwards out of the game.

His judgment was sound because Mark went on to win 73 Welsh caps. His record marks him out clearly as one of United's greats but his value went far beyond statistics. Just to see Mark Hughes muscling around up front inspired team-mates and supporters alike. You knew the opposing defenders would have their work cut out. Mark started 448 games, all at the highest level, for United and scored 162 goals. He is up there with the best.

We have become good friends as our careers have progressed, side by side at times, and I was very pleased to become Mark's assistant when he was appointed the manager of Wales. Incidentally, I am the first Englishman to hold that post, to which I have been made very welcome - but more about that later.

Gradually I began to impose my coaching philosophies on the Old Trafford youth set-up. That meant great emphasis was placed upon ball work. During my playing days, I had often felt deeply frustrated by some of the approaches of managers and coaches and most infuriating of all was when the ball was kept away from players in training.

Make no mistake, lower division players have got skill and can show it if they are encouraged to do so. That encouragement never used to be forthcoming. Come the game on Saturday though we would get the usual instructions. "Don't take chances at the back - belt it upfield if there is any hint of danger. Defenders, play the ball long. Don't risk playing into midfield. Midfielders, don't get caught in possession. Never try to turn with the ball. Play the way you are facing or hook the ball forward."

You were a nervous wreck before you went out to play. After hardly seeing a ball in training all week, when a match arrived you were ordered to get rid of it as soon as you could.

Whenever Saturday came along, the fear factor crept in. The manager insisted you take no risks whatsoever and good players were quickly reduced to bad ones. Most footballers do what the manager says and they don't want to let anyone down but they are letting themselves down because a lot of lower division players could perform at a much higher level given the right encouragement. A perfect example is Dion Dublin.

Dion was later to join Manchester United from Cambridge United in the second half of the 1991/92 season. He had scored 53 goals in 156 games for Cambridge as, under John Beck's ugly but temporarily effective long-ball style (I'll come back to long-ball later), they rose from the old Fourth Division to the Second. Dion had spent years labouring under long-ball tactics and endured training session upon training session without kicking a ball.

John Beck's favoured style of play was everything I abhor but, to be fair, he could spot the basics in a player and Dion had all the basics. Alex Ferguson signed him for United for £1.1 million after being alerted to his potential from a videotape of his goals sent to us by Beck.

In one of our training sessions, not long after he arrived, Dion gave one of the younger players a rollicking for not shouting to him "Man on". That means that the young player was supposed to warn Dion that a defender was close by when he received the ball. I immediately pulled Dion to one side and asked him: "Have you got a pair of eyes?" "Of course I have," said Dion. So I told him to use them and look over his shoulder then he would see for himself where the defender marking him was. Dion had to learn something that every kid at Manchester United has to learn from their first days at the club. It is called awareness. Be aware for yourself and your team-mates' benefit. Never offload responsibility.

Dion promptly apologised to the kid, which was typical of him. He is one of the nicest men that I have ever met. When Dion left United to join Coventry City in a £2 million deal in September 1994 I was surprised because he still had to improve some aspects of his game. His progress at Old Trafford had been badly hindered by a horrible injury sustained in a collision with Crystal Palace's defender Eric Young. No blame could be attached to Eric but Dion was left with a fractured leg and badly damaged ligaments.

He never really got much chance in the United first team after he returned to fitness and when he moved to Coventry I did not think he would become an England player. The value of his two-and-a-half years at United then became clear though as he improved further and had a great spell at Highfield Road, before going on to Aston Villa. I thought Dion was unlucky to be left out of England's World Cup squad for France '98. His game has improved so much that he can operate as a central defender as well as a top class striker.

Dion has always been a footballer fully committed to his profession and that devotion probably earned him his chance at international level. He is very much in the mould of David Platt and Gary Neville; plenty of dedication and character which has lifted them to the top of their tree. I thought that Manchester United would have been Dion's finishing school but it wasn't to be. What he learned with us, though, prepared him for his rise to the very top.

6.

Turning good into great

WHEN I JOINED MANCHESTER UNITED in 1981, there were some very good youth-team players at the club but few really outstanding ones. That situation changed rapidly after Alex Ferguson arrived in November 1986.

Alex had done tremendous things on a small budget at Aberdeen. He produced some great young players and somehow forced the relatively modest Dons, in their football outpost up in north-east of Scotland, to the forefront of a Scottish scene dominated so completely for so long by Rangers and Celtic.

Down in the north-west of England, Bobby Charlton had noticed what Alex Ferguson was achieving and became one of the main advocates of Alex becoming the new United manager. United is a huge club and it would require a huge personality to hoist them to heights comparable to those achieved by his famous predecessors. Bobby sensed that Alex was such a man. And he was right.

Alex Ferguson took over when United were in the bottom half of the First Division and within days had stamped his authority on every corner of his new domain. For those of us involved with the youngsters, his arrival was manna from heaven. It did not surprise me when the Boss made it perfectly clear to every member of staff that the way forward for the club was in producing our own players. Yes, you could always strengthen your squad through the transfer market but the squad had to be based on a rolling production-line of home-grown talent. Although we had done pretty well, he said, we were miles short of perfection. United, he insisted, were the great under-achievers.

I thought that he was having a go at me. Probably being a little sensitive I told him: "Get me some better material to work with and I will produce more first team players for you." He took the message on board.

The Boss arrived at Old Trafford accompanied by his assistant from Aberdeen, Archie Knox. Both had the same temperament - fiery, with a capital F. A whirlwind hit Manchester United from day one.

There was an abundance of passion, enthusiasm and motivation around but it was not all just "gung-ho." A lot of serious thinking and planning was going on too. The Boss has excellent skills in spotting natural football talent - just look at the number of home-produced players in Manchester United's squad in the last 10 years. He is also very supportive of his staff and prepared to listen to their opinions before making his own judgement.

Alex's ferocity did not worry me. I had dealt with Brian Clough, after all, and had always been mentally strong where football was concerned. One Saturday morning however, a situation got a little out of hand.

My youth team were playing Burnley at our training ground, the Cliff. If the first team were playing at home, the boss and Archie always watched the kids - I have been in football well over 40 years and I have never met two harder working men. The boss was watching the game as usual from his office upstairs and I was watching from the coach's room next door. This was my usual practice because I got a perfect view from there.

We were winning the game, only 1-0 but quite comfortably,

when suddenly Archie came flying through the door and got stuck into me. He kept shouting; "Can your forwards only play one-twos around the box? Haven't they got any other ideas?" Archie did not realise that I could be as volatile as him and I forgot all about the game and launched back at him. He retorted by saying that he thought we were a very poor team (though 'poor' was not the exact word used.) He said the youth team at Aberdeen would beat us 6-0. That was like a red rag to a bull and I told him get Aberdeen down here so we could see.

It was a right old up-and-downer and the Boss had to come out of his office to calm us both down. It just showed the incredible passion at the club; a determination to win at whatever level. Players and coaches quickly got the message; 100 per cent effort was demanded at all times, in matches and in training.

I got to know Archie Knox more quickly than I did the boss. This is the usual way in football because coaches spend a lot more time together. I grew to like Archie because he was my kind of man. He was passionate about football, worked hard and loved a night out for relaxation. It took me longer to get to know the gaffer but I quickly realised what he wanted on the football side; 24 hours-a-day commitment to Manchester United. This was fine by me because I was desperate to be successful as youth team manager. After a playing career spent at outposts of the League on the books of clubs which were struggling to exist, never mind succeed, here was my chance to enjoy success with one of the biggest clubs in the world.

As I settled in at Old Trafford I thought many, many times about the Busby Babes. My mission was to try to develop a generation of young players to be just as good. I had heard all about the work that Jimmy Murphy, who nurtured the Busby generation, had done and the success he had achieved. It was the hardest possible act to follow. The older supporters had a story every day for me about Busby and Murphy and later on I was to be extremely proud when both Matt and Jimmy complimented me on the job that I was doing.

Praise from people inside the game - people who really know what's involved - means most of all. It was pleasing to read in David Beckham's book, "My Story", that Bryan Robson believes I have been the most successful worker with the young since Jimmy Murphy. The much-misunderstood Beckham - more of him later - was also very generous when he referred to me as the greatest youth team coach in the country.

Back to those early days, though, and after the Boss had examined, with his usual professionalism and precision, my personality and coaching ability, I finally got to know him. I respected him for what football meant to him and for what Manchester United meant to him. Fifteen years on I feel that we are now good friends and I tease him that he is much softer with players than in his initial seasons.

The Boss really got his teeth into the youth policy and as a result the scouting system was revamped and expanded. United employ about 30 scouts who receive a basic wage and expenses. They are very dedicated, highly-motivated people who get out and about on touch-lines all over the country in all weathers. An umbrella is often their only shelter from the elements as they scour the ranks of junior football searching among all the triers and the dreamers for that rare youngster with something special.

All the scouts were called together and the Boss spelled out to them that without good scouts, Manchester United could not become as successful as he wanted. He told them that to become a good scout it was necessary to go out in all weathers, possess patience and have an eye for spotting young players. He urged them to remember that wherever they were, they were always representing Manchester United. Most of what he told them, of course, they already knew but it was clever stuff. He made them feel important, no, vital to his ambitions. They were - scouts keep a football club's lifeblood circulating - but it never does anyone any harm to be complimented and they went away more committed than ever to unearthing a great generation of United players.

The Boss's heavy involvement in scouting and youth development acted as a great spur to our young players. He tried to watch all the trials, spoke at length to the boys and their parents and made them feel that Manchester United was the only club they wanted to represent.

Not long after Alex became manager, I bumped into Brian Kidd who had just returned to England after several years playing in America. I knew Brian from my coaching days at Everton where he had been a striker in the late 1970s and we always got on very well. We happened to meet up again at a time when United were short-staffed for evening coaching sessions at the Cliff. I was finding it difficult to cope on the two nights each week when the schoolboys came in for training.

Ray Wood, a schoolteacher and good friend of mine, had been assisting me. For many years Ray had scouted for Charlton Athletic and, knowing his ability, I was delighted when he agreed to do some coaching but sadly, after a short illness, he died. It was a devastating blow to his family, the club and myself.

The vacancy, so tragically created, occurred just when Brian Kidd arrived back in the country and he was very keen to join. All our young players knew that Brian had been a famous player for United. Here was a guy who had shared a dressing-room with Best, Charlton, Law, Crerand, Stepney and Stiles. He had been there and done it and that meant the boys were eager to listen and try to emulate him.

Brian was very surprised to learn that we were missing out on signing some of the local boys and later on, when he became youth development officer, he made sure that situation was addressed. Brian knew all the youth leagues, built brilliant contacts and put the wheels into action to make sure that we had scouts at all the key youth games in Greater Manchester. Brian was determined to increase the balance of local youngsters coming our way because at the time Manchester City were outdoing us.

The boss soon realised that Brian was a major asset to the club and brought him onto the full-time staff. Brian and I worked together many, many hours on the training ground. On Saturdays, I looked after the A team and he looked after the B team. The A's included mainly older apprentices and young professionals with the occasional first-team player on the way back after long absences. Bryan Robson and Gordon Strachan both used A team games on the way back from serious injury.

Bryan always took a big interest in youngsters coming through and, even at the height of his career, often came to watch the youth team training at the Cliff. Much later, he was to offer me a coaching position at Middlesbrough but he understood that I could not leave Old Trafford because I wanted to see many of my young players - Ryan Giggs, David Beckham, the Nevilles, Paul Scholes and Nicky Butt - establish themselves in the first team. Bryan's offer was very gratifying, as it was to hear him state that my education on the training pitch was why so many of today's stars at Old Trafford have such good habits. He recognised that I always wanted lads to enjoy football. I wish him all the best in his management career.

When the FA Youth Cup came around, I was in charge of the team, assisted by Brian Kidd. We worked very well together. I obviously had more coaching experience and I think I helped to develop him as an excellent coach. He shared my insatiable thirst for knowledge and improvement and was always asking questions. We never stopped talking about coaching problems and spinning ideas off each other.

When Brian was promoted to youth development officer, a replacement had to be found. A legend arrived in the shape of Nobby Stiles, returning to the club where he had enjoyed some of the finest moments of his great career. Nobby came with a mass of coaching and management experience as manager of Preston North End, and coach at Preston, Vancouver Whitecaps and West

The View From the Dugout

Bromwich Albion.

Nobby took over the B team, which usually comprised younger apprentices and schoolboys and during the week we worked together. A lovely man to work with, Nobby has a great sense of humour. All the youngsters looked forward to sessions with him. We formed a great partnership, similar to Brian and myself. I enjoyed working with both of them and Nobby was kind enough to speak at my retirement dinner. He has now retired from coaching but is in big demand, worldwide, as an after-dinner speaker. Incidentally, I remember when Michael Knighton, later owner of Carlisle United, was interested in buying Manchester United, he met the coaching staff and was totally starstruck at meeting Nobby and Brian. The short meeting he held with us was a joke. I thought he was a fool then and when he ran out on to the pitch and kicked a ball out towards the Stretford End, that confirmed by view. Thank heaven he didn't buy the club!

Now the wheels were really in motion to improve our intake of schoolboys. Brian is a man with strong opinions and a willingness to express them and he ruffled a few feathers amongst the scouts. That obviously did the trick because we started to get better quality youngsters.

We had already signed Ryan Giggs, who played for Salford Boys. Let me put the record straight about his Manchester City connection. He had nothing binding with City so we invited him down for training which we were perfectly entitled to do. Ryan liked our organisation and stayed.

It was easy to see, very early on, that he had got the most amazing talent and, it transpired, he had the discipline and desire to make the most of it. Wales, of whom I am now assistant manager, have benefited from his remarkable ability. It's ironic that I, along with another of my Old Trafford products Mark Hughes, should now be trying to get the best out of Ryan for Wales because, years earlier, I tried everything I knew to persuade him to play for England.

48

Under Brian Kidd, our scouts at United did a magnificent job. As well as Giggs we signed Nicky Butt, Paul Scholes, Ben Thornley, Gary Neville, Phil Neville, Chris Casper, John O'Kane and David Johnson. One of our Irish scouts sent us Keith Gillespie but the most pleasing aspect was the infusion of high-quality local boys.

It was one of our London scouts though, Michael Fidgeon, who told us about a boy called David Beckham. David lived in East London, right in the heart of West Ham territory but, luckily for us, his father was a Manchester United supporter. I thought that it would be very difficult to sign David because he was training at Tottenham Hotspur - his grandfather was a Spurs supporter - alongside the likes of Sol Campbell. In July 1991 we tempted him to United and he became part of what I reckon is the best youth team English football has ever produced.

Much later, in his book "My Story", David Beckham said that if your youth team is winning tournaments, you know the club's got an exciting future. It is no wonder, then, that Manchester United is now the best club in the country. He was part of a youth team to treasure.

7.

The best youth team ever

I FOUND MYSELF IN AN UNBELIEVABLY fortunate position. Here was Eric Harrison, formerly of Halifax, Hartlepool, Barrow, Southport and Scarborough, now at the biggest club in the world at a time when they had a whole crop of excellent youngsters coming through. The most exciting group of young players I have ever worked with were there before my eyes.

It was up to me to mould them together into a unit but it was a huge advantage to have such 24-carat raw-material to work with. Ask any chef and he will tell you that the right way to start producing a great recipe is to have the best ingredients. We had them in these fine young players and they all had one thing in common - an incredible determination to succeed.

Just like myself, they wanted to win on every conceivable occasion. Many people in the game say that it does not matter whether young teams win or lose. That is rubbish because winning builds confidence and improves attitude, which are essential factors to the make-up of a professional footballer.

Manchester United's youth team unveiled an amazing catalogue of success in the years ahead. Between 1981 and 1998 we won the Lancashire League Division One title 11 times and were runners-up three times. We won the FA Youth Cup twice and were finalists on three other occasions. It is my firm belief that winning is important at youth level - as long as you play the correct way - but your principles have to be right. These principles are play together as a team, which means respect each other, work your socks off and get stuck in but always attempt to play football where it should be played; on the grass and not in the sky.

Bobby Charlton came to watch as many youth team games as possible and was a hugely important figure in the development of our players. Bobby has always been a constant source of inspiration to myself and United's youngsters. We always knew how much he was behind us. He would watch youth games at the Cliff and also away from home whenever possible. You cannot put a value on that level of commitment and involvement from someone of such stature.

To see the first team manager and Sir Bobby watching our youth games was a huge incentive for us. It made the young players feel important. You can imagine them going home to tell their parents about the game and how excited they would be to say they had been watched by the the top men. To see a couple of legends on the touch-line reminded the youngsters that they belonged to one of the greatest football clubs in the world. It also sent out the most positive messages to parents who knew how committed the club was, all the way down from the very top to its youngsters.

Apart from working on the training ground dealing with young players in group situations, I spent a lot of time talking individually with them. This to me is vitally important because youngsters may not speak in front of a group but they will always talk on a one-to-one basis. From a coach's point of view, this is great preparation.

In these talks I was always very positive. For instance, if I genuinely thought that a young player had any chance of making it all the way to the first team, I would tell him when he was 16 or 17. Gary

The View From the Dugout

Neville's eyes nearly popped out of his head when I told him, aged 16, that he was future first-team material. He did not have the full self-belief that is so important until he heard that from me.

Gary had thought, when he was 11 and 12, that he might not make the grade at all but his outstanding dedication and ability to read the game made him develop rapidly between 13 and 14. He became a natural leader. By the time he was 16, I had such confidence in his ability and mental toughness that I made him captain of the youth team. He skippered the FA Youth Cup-winning side of 1992 and formed a superb central defensive partnership with Chris Casper. Gary was a role model of what I wanted out of the team. His ability on the field was similar to mine in a training role. I required someone to organise things on the pitch and he became a mini Tony Adams. I cannot pay Gary a higher compliment because Tony Adams is the best organiser on the field in this country.

I also kept telling Paul Scholes what a good player he was and that he would play in the Manchester United first team but, at first, he too did not seem convinced. A local lad, born in Salford, Paul was always one of the quieter members of the dressing room - what a contrast to his tigerish presence on the pitch! I asked him what was troubling him and he said that he thought he was too small. I quickly told him I was not worried about his size because he was good enough. "If I'm not bothered," I said, "then you definitely shouldn't be." That appeared to calm him down and my prophecy came true yet again.

Paul seized his first-team chance early and emphatically. At the age of just 21 he had a massive influence on our Premiership and FA Cup double-winning season of 1995/96 with 14 goals from just 18 starts. Inevitably, he has forced himself into a regular place in England's midfield and Scotland certainly found out all about his deadly knack of ghosting into space in the opponents' box in the Euro 2000 qualification play-off at Hampden Park. All over the pitch, Paul contributes intelligently. Once we had filled him with the self-belief you need to succeed at top level, there was no stopping him.

Developing players to their full potential is not just about working on the training ground. Discipline off the pitch and respect for each other, on and off the pitch, is vital. A young player has to sacrifice a lot away from the football field. He cannot be easily led by his mates because this can lead to domestic problems which might affect his playing performance.

It is no good a coach attempting to get the players supremely fit if they are drinking and staying out late at night. They have got to look after their bodies. Our dietician, Trevor Lee, makes sure that they eat the right food and that their liquid intake is correct. Alcohol is definitely off the agenda. All this is good advice and wasted if the young boys misbehave off the pitch. If they do misbehave, they are idiots and I have no time for them. To have talent and not to maximise it, when you think of all the boys who would love to be professional footballers but are not good enough, is a crime.

Generally our young players are sensible and responsible. This, for sure, is because they know that if they are good enough the boss will give them their chance in the first team. That is an unbelievable motivating factor for the boys.

The Manchester United youth team of 1991 included Gary Neville, John O'Kane, Phil Neville, Chris Casper, David Beckham, Keith Gillespie, Nicky Butt, Paul Scholes, Ben Thornley, Robert Savage, Joe Roberts and Kevin Pilkington. They played the best football I have seen a youth team play as individually and collectively they came along very quickly. Ryan Giggs was already in the first team and playing brilliantly and I couldn't wait for some of the other boys to join him at the senior level.

Saturday mornings were always a joy and 11am on a Saturday could not come round quickly enough. I should have put the players on crowd bonuses because you could hardly find a space to stand at the Cliff, the United training ground where we played all our home games.

None of the professional clubs charge their supporters to watch their junior teams - we are very pleased when fans turn up to watch. The Manchester Evening News, the United match programme and word of mouth gave us very much-needed publicity and our fans turned up in droves. They knew then that they were watching first-team players of the future. Paul Scholes even used to have his own fan club. What a favourite he was with the supporters! He gave us some unbelievable goals to savour. I remember him scoring after beating half of the Liverpool A team. He received a fantastic ovation.

I could not contain my excitement at watching these young stars train and play and I was always speaking to the boss, telling him how good they were. He was already very familiar with them because he watched as many of their games as possible and he also watched them in training whenever he had the time. I used to nag at the boss, saying: "When are you going to give them a chance in the first team?" His answer was always; "Trust me, I will give them their chance."

"Trust me" are the two words he always used with the parents of young lads we were trying to sign. You can trust Sir Alex Ferguson. The boss was true to his word.

When he sold Andrei Kanchelskis, Mark Hughes and Paul Ince in the summer of 1995, many of the supporters thought that he was crazy but he was convinced that my boys were good enough to replace them. He told me that I had got my wish and put most of them in the team for the opening game of the 1995/96 season against Aston Villa at Villa Park. The team that day was: Schmeichel, Parker, Irwin, G Neville, Pallister, Sharpe, Butt, Keane, McClair, Scholes, P Neville. David Beckham was among the substitutes.

That afternoon I was scouting at Barnsley and at half-time the scores from all round the country were broadcast over the tannoy. The Premiership scores came through and I would have thought that Aston Villa v Manchester United would be first out but I was left sweating because they left it until the last. The Yorkshire voice boomed out over the tannoy: Aston Villa 3 Manchester United 0. I thought the stand roof was going to come off with the noise of the fans. My heart sank. I found it hard to concentrate on the second half. On my way home in the car, I heard that we had scored and it had appeared that we had played a little better in the second half. Beckham went on and got a goal but nevertheless the final score was 3-1 to Villa.

I can't remember whether it was that night on Match of the Day, or a little later, when Alan Hansen came out with his famous comment that no team can win anything with kids. What a howler! Well, after the Villa game, we won the next five league games - at home to West Ham, Wimbledon and Bolton and away to Blackburn and Everton - on the bounce and lost just one of the next 17. And, of course, we went on to win the title that season.

If anyone should have known how good our "kids" were it was Hansen. Only a season or two earlier, on his way back from injury, he had played as an over-age player for Liverpool's A team in a Lancashire League game against our A team at The Cliff. Many of the kids who he said would win nothing were in the team that opposed him and we won 6-1. We produced a great display with Hansen assisting us with one of the finest own goals I have ever seen.

Win nothing with kids? Depends on the "kids" doesn't it? I always thought that the BBC staff researched better than that.

8.

Giggs & Co.

A LOT OF PEOPLE HAVE ASKED ME who is the best player I have helped to develop and the truthful answer is I still don't know after all these years. Players have so many different attributes it is really impossible to compare.

Ryan Giggs, when he is in full flight, is probably the most exciting player. I have always encouraged him to run with the ball because of his skill. A player like Ryan is crucial to a successful team. Passing is always a vital ingredient but it is not enough from a team at the top level - someone has got to run with the ball and Ryan Giggs, along with David Ginola and Steve McManaman, is up there with the best in Europe. Players who have pace and can dribble at speed excite any follower of football.

When Ryan joined United on a full-time basis from school - he had signed schoolboy forms with us on his 14th birthday in 1987 - I quickly told him that I was going to play him in a lot of games as a striker. He replied that he had never really played there and asked why was I going to do that. I said that when I had watched him play for Salford Boys against St. Helens Boys in the final of the English Schools Cup he was in his usual left-wing position and, because of the lack of service, hardly got a kick. I explained to him that in my games, he would be constantly involved because with his ability it would be a crime if he was not on the ball all the time. I also said that playing as a striker, he would learn the game much quicker. You need to produce more movement as a striker than as a winger. Forwards need to move without the ball more, which was a skill that Ryan was lacking.

As a bright lad, Ryan readily agreed to switch his position. A great student, he was always eager to learn and prepared to try anything which would get him into the first team quicker than he had anticipated.

There were two things on which he really needed to improve and we both worked hard on them. One, as I have mentioned, was his running off the ball. The other was his right foot. Working hard was no problem to Ryan because he loved it. He was then, and is now, a smashing person with a fabulous personality. He is an excellent ambassador for any youngster to emulate.

I improved Ryan's right foot by making him practice in crossing sessions with it and restricting his left foot to about only ten per cent of the sessions. It was a bit like an optician putting an eye-patch over a child's good eye to make the "lazy eye" work harder. Ryan's right foot was forced to deal with the ball rather than just support his right leg - and it worked.

I always felt that Ryan Giggs needed challenging. He has unbelievable natural talent and he is such a great athlete. I believed that with those attributes he could be asked to do almost anything on the football field.

When Ryan was 15 I took him with United's under 18s to a very tough tournament in Italy. I played him in all the games, and expected him to perform well in all of them. He was already, in my eyes, a first-team player of the near future.

Some coaches insist that young players should be allowed to develop slowly. I take a very different attitude. If I am convinced that I have a youth team player who is going to be good enough for the first team, I push him along quickly. I put him through the mangle and I expect him to survive every challenge.

This Italian tournament was a huge test for Ryan. At half-time in one of the games I gave him a bit of a rollicking because I was not satisfied with his contribution. Ryan was stung by my criticisms of him and his face told me everything.

A little while later Brian Kidd, who was my assistant, beckoned me over to him and he said that he thought I was out of order with my attitude towards Ryan. "Remember he is only fifteen," he said. I would not back down and told Kiddo that I expected Ryan to play in United's first-team in the very near future. He was heading for the big league and would have to get used to receiving a rollicking from time to time.

Young players come across many obstacles on the way up in football. They must remember that professional football is not an industry for soft lads. It is tough to get to the top and even tougher to stay there. In all honesty to Ryan, he has always accepted fair criticism. He always knew that, from a schoolboy, I cared about him and everything I did was for his benefit. Ryan is mentally very strong and has plenty of bottle and I now thoroughly enjoy working with him in my capacity of assistant manager of Wales.

I cannot visualise Ryan ever playing for any other club because he loves Manchester United so much but after his playing career I can see him becoming a good coach.

Even after he became established in the first-team, Ryan remained heavily involved with the club's young players. When the first-team players are working on possession in training, they sometimes split up into two groups; the old men and the young lads. Ryan is always with the young players and is a tremendous help to them. They really respect him and he has inspired many youngsters. He was in the first team at an early age, and the kids watched him and thought that they could eventually follow him into the senior side. The manager had given Ryan an early chance and he had seized it. It supplied further proof of what all the young players knew - that Alex Ferguson would give them an opportunity if they delivered the goods in the junior teams.

Ryan began helping me more and more with the youth team squad and became, in effect, my assistant. That is the way we do it at Manchester United. We help each other and we pump confidence into each other. I constantly tell young players to respect each other and to develop their own team spirit. The dressing room on training days is their second home and I rarely went into it from Monday to Friday because they grow up together in there.

Gary Neville has been at the club since he was 11 so I have worked with him for many years. I am the first to admit that, for the first two years, I did not think he would make the grade. He had the basic skills but was not technically good enough. Between 13 and 14, I was changing my mind because he was working so hard to improve his ability. At 16 I made him captain of the youth team. This was unusual because normally I would give the job to a 17 or 18-year-old who would be more mature. Nevertheless, I was certain that Gary would be a first-team player and an international footballer.

There is no more dedicated player in English football than Gary. He is a fine example to any aspiring youngster who wants to become a professional footballer. His concentration and reading of the game is second to none. He is a credit to himself and to his football mad family. His father - Neville Neville! - is the commercial manager of Bury, currently in the Nationwide League Division Two, and his mother Jill is club secretary at Gigg Lane. Gary and David Beckham have always been good friends and it was no surprise to me when Gary was best man at the Beckham's wedding in Ireland. He carried out his duties meticulously and did an excellent job which I witnessed at first hand.

Phil Neville is a couple of years younger than Gary and, as a 12 and 13-year-old, was a better player than his elder brother had been at those ages. Nowadays there is not a lot to choose between them but Gary's experience possibly tips the scales at the moment. Phil is a fine footballer but will be even better. At this stage of his career he just lacks a bit of confidence. Missing out on England's squad for the 1998 World Cup did not help him.

When he matures, he will be a regular with United and England. From what I can gather, if he had chosen cricket as a career he would probably now be playing regularly for Lancashire and many experts reckon he may have gone on to play for England. He played for Lancashire at under 11, under 13 and under 15 age groups and made his debut for Lancashire 2nd XI at just 15 years of age. Thankfully for United, he chose to concentrate on the big round ball game rather than the little one. His sister Tracey plays netball for England as a striker. Their sports-mad parents, Neville and Jill, must wake up every day thinking it's Christmas!

Paul Scholes, like Phil Neville, was also a more than useful cricketer. He never ceases to amaze me with the things he does on the football pitch. I should not be amazed really because I have seen him do those things regularly since the age of 16. At that age, Paul reminded me of Kenny Dalglish. That is a massive compliment because Dalglish was one of the best British players I have ever seen. His similarity with Dalglish is that he always seems to have eyes in the back of his head. He always seems to know where every player is on the pitch and which direction they are moving in. That means he can read the game brilliantly and assess the angles to split even the tightest of defences with a single pass.

In front of goal, Scholes is deadly. He can score any type of goal. Just like Dalglish, too, he can also look after himself on the pitch. He is the quiet man of the young ones but very good company when you get to know him and a lovely, kind-hearted person. I can remember him agreeing, without a moment's hesitation, to visit a special needs school in Halifax for me, together with Ryan Giggs.

Scholes' big pal, Nicky Butt, is a totally different character. Boisterous and exuberant - it's a case of what you see is what you get with Nicky. He was the first to break through into the first team from that group of excellent youngsters which it was my privilege to coach. It was not surprising really because he always had fantastic fitness, courage and an incredible will to win. I have always likened him to Bryan Robson and, like Robbo, he is not afraid of anyone. No player will ever be able to bully Nicky out of the game. Robbo certainly shares my high opinion of Nicky. When Bryan left Old Trafford for Middlesbrough in 1994, he pinpointed Butt as the best prospect of all those coming through the Old Trafford system.

I am puzzled why Nicky does not score more goals. Like Robson he is very good in the air and his ability to find space in the penalty area, and get into positions to head for goal, is excellent. Perhaps the goals will come in the future. He needs to score more goals to become a regular member of the England team but if I was playing in the roughest, most intimidating of games, I would want Nicky by my side.

And then there is David Beckham. He can do absolutely anything with a football. Perhaps it is not surprising that his skills are breathtaking as he has always seemed to have a ball at his feet since I first knew him as a schoolboy. If anybody out there thinks that all that the things David has accomplished have just landed in his lap then they could not be more wrong. Ever since his formative years, he has practised from morning until night. As the old song says, to be the best, dedication is what you need. You won't find anybody more dedicated than David.

It is vital for kids to practice hard as soon as they are old enough to put a pair of boots on. My young grandsons Connor and Joseph were kicking a ball around as soon as they could walk.

David had to be nursed along a bit between the ages of 16 to 17 because his physique was changing dramatically. He literally shot up in size. The stamina was still there - believe you me, David can run all day - but the strength was not. He was frustrated at not progressing as fast as some of the other lads. As always, I was constantly talking to the boys, one-to-one, and I think that these chats helped David. He has always been a little sensitive but a brilliant lad to work with.

When David started getting stronger, he really blossomed. We now had a midfield player who had all the skill in the world, who could run for fun and had the physique to go with it. Quickly he had been transformed from a small, skinny kid to a six-footer with broad shoulders. We were now seeing the David Beckham that I had always visualised.

Many people seem surprised when he hits a 40-yard pass or bends a 25-yard free-kick into the top corner of the net. In youth team matches, if we got a free-kick 25 yards from goal, I used to be disappointed if he did not score. That was because I saw him practicing free-kicks every day in training. He came back voluntarily when I took the under 16s after school and that would be his third training session of the day.

He was not alone. Gary and Phil Neville were usually with him. Young players at Manchester United are on the training ground and in the gymnasium, morning, afternoon and sometimes evenings. If they fail to reach the first team, it's not through the lack of trying.

David Beckham deserves all the success he has achieved so far and there is more to come in the future, believe me. I am emphasising this because of all the disgraceful abuse he gets from opposing fans. This obviously stems from his red card against Argentina in the World Cup in 1998 and also his marriage to Posh Spice. He has to tolerate an awful lot of horrible, pathetic abuse from mindless morons but nevertheless he never turns down a polite request for his autograph. He is always pleasant with decent people and is very popular with all his team-mates.

People criticise his wife, Victoria, but I have spoken to her on many occasions and she is a lovely girl. Pleasant, down to earth, no airs and graces. I remember asking David to go to a children's hospital to visit some sick children when, out of the blue, my telephone rang at home. It was David to talk about the visit. We chatted and then he said that Victoria would like a word. She came on the phone and asked if she could go to the hospital with David. Before I could answer, she said that she would not be offended if they just wanted David.

I replied that they would be absolutely thrilled if she was there too. Consequently they both went to the hospital, to the kids delight, and stayed there much longer than expected. The next day I received a telephone call from the charity organiser and he said that David and Victoria were just fantastic with the kids. That shows that these two superstars are just ordinary decent people who happen to have special talents. I wish that a small, disgusting minority of football fans would realise that and let them get on with their lives.

It was very flattering to read in David's book, "My Story," that he rates me the best youth team coach in the country. He said I taught him all the right things and encouraged him when things were not going well. That just goes to prove what a superb person he is, with his feet on the ground and not forgetting the people who helped shape his career. It was a lovely gesture of him and Victoria to invite Shirley and myself to their wedding. I was thrilled when David achieved yet another milestone by captaining his country, against Italy in Turin in November 2000.

Wesley Brown is a player who can definitely follow my former young players into the full England team. His biggest asset is his pace and added to that is great stamina. These days, good athletes are the flavour of the month and Wes is certainly a superb athlete. I feel sure that he could have had a great career in athletics. I can remember Peter Schmeichel watching one of my running sessions. I had all the young players doing eight 200-metre timed runs and Peter gasped when he saw Wes flying round the course. Wes is a magnificent sight in full flight and even though he was only 16 at the time, Peter said that anyone who could run like that must be a future first-team player. I assured Peter that Wes could play a bit as well.

The View From the Dugout

He needs to work on his passing and his positional play. If he does that, he will get to the top of his profession. Unfortunately, a serious injury interrupted Wes's development but I am convinced that will only make him more determined to succeed. If Wes keeps listening and learning, he will play in the United first team on a regular basis and add to his one England cap. He will certainly not be a one-cap wonder.

John Curtis is another player for whom I have great hopes. Like Wes Brown he is a flying-machine, which is vitally important in today's high-speed football. Originally a central defender, John switched to full-back partly due to the fact that he did not reach beyond 5ft 9in tall. He is a first-class man-to-man marker. I would fancy his chances against any attacker.

I always fancied John to mark Michael Owen out of the game - and you don't get a much higher compliment than that. John and Michael played against each other many times when they were both at the National School of Excellence at Lilleshall, in Shropshire. They both know each other's game very well - but John usually had the edge.

One man who did give him a torrid time, though, was Arsenal's Marc Overmars in the 1998 Premiership game at Old Trafford. The Dutchman was his master that day but, as a 19-year-old, John learned from the experience. I spoke to him the following day and he admitted that he had been taken to the cleaners but, typical of his confidence, said that he wished he could play against Overmars again the following Saturday.

Unfortunately, his chances of advancement at Manchester United were limited but I am not surprised that Blackburn Rovers have paid £1.5 million for his service. It was pleasing to read in the "Lancashire Evening Post" that he did not think he could have gone to any other football club in the world and collected the experience and football education he gained at Old Trafford. Comments like that from the players - the people it is really all about - bring back happy memories of my time at the Cliff. I have still retained my links with Manchester United because I coach the schoolboys two evenings a week, and scout in a part-time capacity for the club.

It is the best club in the world. I remember all those mornings spent standing there on the touch-line discussing with those great men Alex Ferguson and Bobby Charlton the prospects for players like Ryan Giggs and David Beckham. Sometimes I had to pinch myself. Could all this really have happened to the teenage hopeful from Hebden Bridge? Miss Copley - sometimes it's right to aim high!

9.

Cantona and other foreign influences

THROUGHOUT MY CAREER, I have always talked to as many managers, coaches and players as possible to gather as much knowledge as I could to enable me to become a better coach.

You must have a vast store of knowledge to survive in the football jungle and you must always be receptive to ideas. Some you take on board; others you discard, but listening to start off with never hurt anybody. And when English football started taking in more and more players from abroad I identified a whole new source of knowledge to plunder. I was quick to embrace their influence.

Four foreign players, in particular, fascinated me. To Old Trafford from four different European countries came Eric Cantona, Arnold Muhren, Peter Schmeichel and Andrie Kanchelskis to illuminate Manchester with their considerable and very different skills and attributes. This was a heaven-sent opportunity for me. Different approaches. New ideas. I spent a great deal of my time talking to them. I wanted to know how they were nurtured and prepared as young players, who and what had influenced them and basically everything about their - and their country's - philosophy towards football.

As soon as Eric Cantona arrived at Manchester United in

1992, I wanted to kidnap him and spend a week talking to him about football. I bided my time though because it was a hectic period following his move from Leeds United. I let him settle in before I approached him but when I did, I found him extremely receptive. Eric is not only a great footballer with superb skills but a very nice man. He was always polite and accommodating and, for such a high-profile player, that was incredible.

I asked Eric if there was a difference between my coaching philosophy and the French way. He said the two were quite similar. I also asked him if our young players at United were on a par with the French youngsters at the top French clubs. He was well qualified to judge having played for some of France's finest including Marseilles, Nantes, Auxerres and Montpelier.

He replied that, ability-wise they were similar but he thought that one aspect of the French boys' game was better than ours; and that was that they received the ball better than our young players. I took that on board straight away and, as always when I have been given good advice, I acted. Plans and ideas are all very well on the drawing-board but they mean nothing unless they are put into - and made to work in - practice.

In this instance, I introduced more juggling with the ball because five to ten minutes of this exercise developed good ball control. Surely, if it was good enough for Cantona, it was good enough for my boys.

When Eric served an eight-month first-team suspension for an incident with a Crystal Palace fan at Selhurst Park in January 1995, he spent quite a lot of time training with my youngsters. Not only did the young players love it, so did I. In seven-a sides and 11-a-sides he always wanted the ball - actually, he quickly became frustrated if the youngsters did not pass to him often enough. I had to encourage the kids to pass the ball to Eric at every opportunity. This was for two reasons. Firstly, the club wanted him sharp as a razor for his return to first-team action. Secondly, it was just great for myself and the boys to see him produce his magical football skills.

I wonder how many fans observed that he rarely passed, crossed or sent in a shot with swerve on the ball. Also he very rarely passed the ball with spin or swerve on it because - his logic was indisputable - it is easier for a team-mate to control a ball that is not spinning.

Some journalists said that the Frenchman was just an individual player and not really a team player. Well, that is utter rubbish. Eric Cantona was a team player but more than that even. A club player. His influence extended beyond the first-team squad. His mere arrival at the training ground was a boost for me and the kids because a world-famous player, at the peak of his career, was happy to spend time with youngsters setting out right at the beginning of theirs. Magnificent.

I am always preaching the value of practicing and there before our eyes was a superstar who practiced properly all the time. Alex Ferguson always speaks about the influence that Cantona had on the young players and he is correct. As kids do, they watched and they copied him. Not only did the kids copy him, I did as well. For instance, every day Eric would juggle with the ball, a practice which we in the game call keep-ups. That became a part and parcel of my daily training routines. If it was good enough for Eric it was good enough for my coaching.

I would love to see Eric Cantona take on a manager's job some day. He has so many diverse interests in life that maybe he won't get round to it but if ever he does I will pay good money to watch one of his teams play. As a profound thinker he would produce a team full of invention and exciting posibilities. I believe that his side would be an attacking one but well-organised. His tactics would be very interesting.

During his career Eric scored some sensational goals. My two favourites are his chip against Sunderland at Old Trafford and the strike which won the F.A. Cup for Manchester United against

Liverpool at Wembley in 1996. The latter was a volley which he had a split second to hit and kept down brilliantly. Only a player of the highest calibre can score such goals. Eric le Magnifique.

The first foreign player I spoke to at length was Arnold Muhren. Arnold was a hugely talented midfield player with enormous experience, so when he joined United I could not wait to grill him. After playing for quite a few years in Holland, he was astutely signed by Ipswich Town manager Bobby Robson. He became part of a fabulous team which had players like Mick Mills, Kevin Beattie, Paul Mariner, John Wark, Alan Brazil and Franz Thijssen. It was a team which played marvellous free-flowing football which made going to play Ipswich at Portman Road a mammoth task for any football club.

Ron Atkinson persuaded Arnold to come to Old Trafford in the summer of 1982 and he immediately enhanced our team. His wonderful left foot could open up the best of defences. Added to his great skills was a terrific personality. Arnold was always pleasant and always approachable. That suited me because I was keen to take the first chance I got to tap into his knowledge.

Arnold was very scathing of teams who did not attempt to play good quality football. I could imagine what he thought whenever he saw defenders launching the ball long and high as soon as they got it. Such a system cuts skilful players like Arnold out of the game. They are reduced to runners - craftsmen turned into labourers. If that is frustrating for anyone watching the match, how do you think the midfielders, especially those blessed with great passing ability like Arnold, feel about it?

As I always preached good quality with my youth team, he was only too pleased to discuss any aspects of the game. He knew that I always stretched the kids and always encouraged them to use their skills in training. Arnold used to call me the "skill master", which delighted me. Both of us possessed a similar football philosophy.

He told me to make sure that none of the young players drank alcohol but I did not need any convincing of that. All the young players already knew that they would be in serious trouble if they transgressed in that way. Looking after your body is absolutely vital, more so than ever because the standards of fitness and pace of play in today's game are so high. The likes of Giggs, Beckham and Scholes have been blessed with wonderful talent but also the intelligence and discipline to live the right life-style off the field. If they did not look after themselves that talent could not flourish.

Arnold Muhren was amazed that some professional footballers drank so much at times. It was not the case at United though. What our players know, of course, is that United has thousands of unofficial 'spotters' out and about every night. Manchester is a football crazy city and the grapevine would rapidly inform me who had been drinking in clubs, pubs or hotels. The club employed a strict disciplinary policy. Anyone who stepped out of line knew they were taking a big risk because we would act immediately to punish anyone caught out.

Arnold and I talked at length about young players being comfortable and relaxed with the ball at their feet. There is a real art to receiving the ball and still be able to see most of your team-mates at the same time. This reminded me of when my youth team played in a tournament in Holland and we played against the Dutch national under 20s team. Amazingly, the Dutch team played the game in almost complete silence. No shouts of "man on", "turn with the ball" or "clear the ball" were heard. They had a picture in their minds of where every player on the field was. This was a great experience for our young players who benefited from that game - as I did as well. My learning process was still in progress of course. It was a question of latching onto every piece of wisdom I could find, honing it in training and bringing the reality into the next game for "hands on" experience.

So far I have spoken about the valuable input of a Frenchman and a Dutchman. Next, one of Scandinavia's finest footballers - the

With the Everton youth team winning a prestigious
international tournament in Germany in 1975. The
captain, Mark Higgins, to my my left, later played for
Everton and Manchester United at first team level.

Two Everton squads of the 1970's.
Above, under Billy Bingham, and below, under
Gordon Lee

**Anything George Best can do, I can do better.
With Miss World, Mary Stavins.**

**Goodison Park will forever be one
of the "special" grounds for me.**

Ron Atkinson
I will forever be grateful to Ron for giving me
the opportunity to coach at Old Trafford.

My wife Shirley with granddaughter Ashleigh
Shirley has been my greatest supporter throughout
my playing and coaching career.

**My daughters, Kim (left) and Vicky (right),
with grandsons Connor and Joseph**

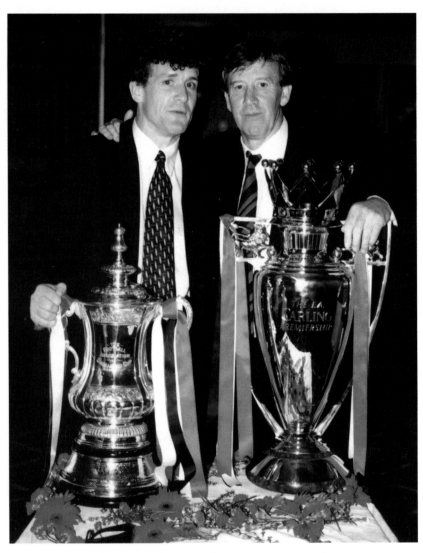

Mark 'Sparky' Hughes with me on one of many great nights at Old Trafford.

Mark was one of my first successes at Old Trafford and it's such a pleasure to be working with him now with the Welsh national team.

great Dane, Peter Schmeichel. He was another player who I chatted to on a regular basis. I was hugely impressed by his mental approach to games. He always thought that we were going to win. No negative thoughts ever appeared to cross his mind.

This kind of thinking is very important in my dealings with the young players at Manchester United. It is more important at Old Trafford than anywhere else because every team wants to beat Manchester United at any level and that imposes a special and unique pressure that our young players have to handle.

People have said to me, "how did the young players cope with Peter Schmeichel ranting and raving at them on the field?" My answer was "no problem" because they had been well brought up at the club. I have a saying to the young players at the Cliff: "Don't let it be a shock to you when you play in the first team." One of the most important parts of my job has been to prepare them for the pressures in the F.A. Carling Premiership.

Peter Schmeichel was a tremendous asset for Manchester United - a very shrewd signing by Alex Ferguson who brought the Great Dane over from Brondby for just £750,000 in August 1991. During his time at Old Trafford he was the best goalkeeper in the world. His presence at the club was huge. He possessed enormous character whilst his goalkeeping skills were unique. These attributes could all be seen whenever he deputised for Roy Keane as captain.

Another very interesting player was Ukrainian-born Andrei Kanchelskis. He was a great winger who played 128 games for United and left a lot of people very disappointed when he departed to join Everton for £5.5 million in 1995. Adored by the fans, Andrei must have been crazy to leave. I can only assume it was for financial gain.

While he was with us I enjoyed Andrei's company a great deal. I talked to him about football when he was a youngster in Russia (Ukraine was then a part of the USSR) and how they developed young players. He attended a sports academy there and spoke about the severe discipline to which the young players were subjected. This was music to my ears again because it is well known at Manchester United that I am a strict disciplinarian. I will argue with anybody if they say that discipline is not important.

Andrei told me that the coaches in his academy insisted that the players played for the team and not just for themselves. He said that if they did not conform, they were out of the team. There was no messing about or second chances! Our young players would not believe what I told them. I got the impression that the Russian coaches were stronger on discipline than even myself, who was known as "Eric the Red."

I got on really well with Andrei but one day he fell out with me. Andrei had to train with me and the kids for some reason - he was probably on his way back from injury. When first-team players trained with the kids, I always told them in advance what we were going to do that day because it showed respect for the senior players. I never changed my routine just because a first-team player was training with us, unless the manager wanted me to do some specific work with them. That was not the case on this occasion so Andrei just had to join in with what I had planned - and he didn't like it.

I told Andrei that we were going to play a game that consisted of a lot of heading and the only way to score a goal was with a header. My group of youngsters were weak where heading was concerned and they needed this practice. Andrei was grumpy straight away. As far as he, out there on the wing, was concerned heading was for someone else to do.

He did not complain although his body language told me that he was not enjoying the session. He got on with it but as we were walking off the training ground at the end, I mischievously asked Andrei whether he had enjoyed the session or not. Well, Andrei was not supposed to speak much English at that time but he certainly did that day.

He exploded into torrents of abuse. "Your session was shit."

"English football is shit." "All you wanted to do today was to kick the ball in the air." That was quite logical, really, considering we were playing to rules which stated that the only way to score a goal was with your head.

At first I laughed it off but then I got a little bit annoyed and Andrei realised this and backed off. I got back to the dressing-room going over in my mind whether I had gone too far by devoting a whole training session to headers. I came to the conclusion that I had done exactly the right thing because I had informed Andrei what I was going to do and that my group, who were my primary responsibility, were weak headers of the ball.

A few minutes later, Andrei appeared at the door with George Scanlon, his interpreter. He was very apologetic and wanted to shake hands, which we did, and it all ended perfectly amicably with respect on both sides.

I have mentioned these four foreign players because I have always thirsted for knowledge and they certainly provided that for me. These days, there are ever-growing influences from all over Europe and beyond in English football and each new country represented in the Premier League has its own way of doing things. The potential for the willing coach to learn and improve himself just grows and grows. I had attended a lot coaching courses in England and derived great benefit from most of them but these continental tips collected here and there offered new insights to the experience and knowledge I was able to pass on to the young players at United.

The current foreign generation at United remain of the highest quality with the likes of Japp Stam, Fabien Barthez and Ole-Gunnar Solskjaer. All are true professionals, totally committed to the pursuit of excellence. Ollie Solskjaer, in particular, is a man I admire for many reasons. Possibly his most admirable feature is his love for and loyalty towards Manchester United.

He will always have a special place in United supporters' hearts. They really adore him. I have criticised some overseas players for their lack of respect for the clubs they play for and the country they play in but in Ollie's case, as with all the foreign players at United, their respect is 100 per cent.

Ollie recalls that when he first left Norway for Old Trafford he was confident of making the grade over here because he had just played for Norway under 21s against England under 21s and done well in a 2-2 draw. He thought he would be on the same level as United's outstanding young players coming through but then began to have second thoughts when he saw them play. Doubts crept into his mind but not into mine. I told him he had no need to worry. United supporters certainly never had any doubts because they took to him straight away.

I don't know who labelled Ollie the 'baby-faced assassin' but whoever it was portayed him spot-on. There are few players in world football who get their body into position to shoot at goal so quickly. When most players would still be getting themselves lined up to shoot, Ollie has pulled the trigger and usually the net is bulging.

Those early doubts when he first arrived in England almost certainly spurred him on to lead a near-perfect lifestyle in terms of attitude and dedication to fitness. He has always ensured that he is 100 per cent fit and ready for training and matches and that means little or no alcohol, a sensible diet and a great desire to be ready, willing and able whenever the call comes in either club or international football.

There are players who fully deserve to be regarded as role models in football and Ollie is certainly one. Another is Chelsea's wonderfully talented striker Gianfranco Zola. I spoke to Gianfranco in November 2000 and it was an uplifting experience. He positively oozes dedication to his chosen career. He has reached the top level by real hard work and determination along, of course, with that inborn talent. He harboured a dream to be a professional footballer and possessed the talent to make that dream a possibility and the dedication to make it a reality.

If I appear to be neglecting the British players then honestly I am not. I am pleased to say that I have gained as much knowledge from them as from the foreign players - and in some cases even more.

A colossus of a player and a great man who is a friend of mine is Bryan Robson. He always inspired me when I watched him play and train. I used him as an example to all the kids and I told them to watch him whenever they could. He was brilliant around the club, always very supportive to me and the kids. He regularly used to watch youth games and we were always discussing their progress and who we thought would eventually make the first team.

Robbo and myself had endless discussions about football and I learned a great deal from him. I told him that he would make a good manager and I think that I have got that one right. When he left Old Trafford to take over the reins at Middlesborough I was very flattered when he asked me to become part of his coaching staff. The main reason why I rejected Bryan's offer was that I wanted to remain at Old Trafford and see many of the youngsters who I had coached come into the first team and go on to become internationals.

It was very kind of Bryan to state that my education on the training pitch was excellent and that he thought that was why so many of United's stars have come through with such good habits. Every time he comes back to Old Trafford he gets a magnificent ovation, which he richly deserves, from our brilliant supporters.

Steve Bruce is another guy who always wants to talk football. As with Robbo, I have had lots of discussions with him. Tactics crop up a lot in discussions with footballers. Some people tend to think that only coaches talk about tactics but believe you me, many players are very good judges on team organisation. After all, from the players of this generation will come the coaches and managers of the next.

The first time I took real note of Steve Bruce was when Alex Ferguson sent me to watch him play in a game for Norwich City at

The View From the Dugout

Everton. We wanted a centre-half and had heard good reports of Steve from our scouts so I was asked to give my opinion on him. That day, Everton murdered Norwich. Steve played quite well but was not outstanding. What really impressed me was what happened at the end of the game. Steve was just as sick as the travelling Norwich fans at being stuffed by Everton. There was a genuine hurt being felt by Steve. That went a long way to me being swayed towards him. I may be doing the rest of the Norwich players a disservice but they did not seem to be hurting as much as Steve.

What a great signing for Manchester United he became. I saw a player with great courage and great character that day at Everton. United fans will never forget his two goals he scored against Sheffield Wednesday at Old Trafford that just about clinched the championship in 1993.

It has always amazed me and many other professional commentators in the game that Steve never collected any England caps. Perhaps we at Old Trafford felt the benefit of that injustice because I think his omission from the England squad spurred him on to better performances for Manchester United.

It is worth remembering that, as a youngster just setting out in the game, Steve had been rejected by Burnley. He did not give up though and ended up starting his professional career with Gillingham, down in Kent, and about as far from home that this native Geordie could get. However, with determination and character he forced his way, via Norwich City, to the top with United.

Burnley said "no thanks" to the teenage Bruce. He ended up skippering Manchester United to the Premiership title. That is an example which should act as a motivating factor for any youngster rejected or released by a professional football club.

10.

The ones who fled the nest

AT EVERY FOOTBALL CLUB, there are cases of the ones that got away. You have a young player at the club, you let him go for one reason or another and he goes on to excel for another club. In other cases, you try to sign a young player and you miss out. Here are three examples of players who almost became part of the Manchester United glory years.

Luck also plays a part sometimes. Take David Platt for instance. In 1982, I took my youth team to Chadderton, a little town just to the north of Oldham, to play a game against their youths. I think it was a fund-raising event for them. We won quite comfortably but I was impressed by one of their strikers, a lad called David Platt. After the match I spoke to the Chadderton manager and told him that I liked the look of David.

I honestly thought that a player of his evident promise must have been tied up with a professional club and that he was helping Chadderton out as a favour. The manager said that wasn't the case - he was just a Chadderton player and no professional club had approached him. I culd hardly believe my luck and asked the manager if he minded if David came to United to attend our evening training sessions. The manager was delighted to oblige so I asked David and he was ecstatic.

When we took a closer look, we liked what we saw. David signed on as an apprentice and was soon impressing in the youth team. He was my kind of player, which is a team player. He ran his socks off for the team - as a striker, remember, not the midfielder he turned out to be - always showing a great attitude. David, though, was and always will be a very shrewd customer and, even as a young man, had a beady eye on the future.

After David's second season at the club, first-team manager Ron Atkinson called him into his office to discuss another contract. David had obviously weighed up the situation and turned down another contract. His valid reasoning was that five players who played in the strikers' positions were in front of him. They were Frank Stapleton, Alan Brazil, Mark Hughes, Norman Whiteside and the late Laurie Cunningham. Even though the latter was on loan at the time from Real Madrid (tragically, soon to lose his life in a car accident in Spain), that left David well down the strikers' pecking order for the immediate future.

Even so, most young players would have jumped at the opportunity of another contract with United but not David. He rejected the contract and asked for a free transfer. Ron Atkinson, as ever a decent man, fully understood David's plight and agreed. Ron even went so far as to alert Dario Gradi, manager of Crewe Alexandra, then in the old Fourth Division, that here was a boy worth taking on. Dario was always on the lookout for young talent and Ron told him to call me. My telephone soon rang and I told him to sign David straight away. If he didn't do it quickly, I warned, David would easily get fixed up with another club.

Dario asked, "Is he that good?" and I replied without hesitation he certainly was. The rest is now history. David Platt played 62 games for England and is now the Nottingham Forest manager. At one point, he was the most expensive player in the world if you calculate all his transfer fees. Aston Villa, Bari, Sampdoria, Juventus.

Not bad for a lad from Chadderton that nobody seemed to want. Being in the right place at the right time, coupled with that essential determination to succeed, can put you on the road to success.

At 13 years of age, David Johnson looked a great prospect. Brian Kidd brought him to Manchester United and said that he thought that David had every chance of making the grade. All the lad's work in the early stages suggested that Brian's opinion was correct. David was progressing very well until he sustained the injury that every footballer fears, worse even than most broken legs; cruciate ligament damage. An operation was carried out and when it was time for rehabilitation - months of tedious, gruelling, gradual recovery - David really struggled to come to terms with it.

Recovering from surgery is one of the toughest tests for a footballer or any professional athlete. Restricted on the physical work they can do, they are unable to get out onto a pitch and do what they are good at. Then there is the boredom of all the necessary fitness work: the treadmill, the running and the hour after hour in the gym. It requires real mental toughness.

David, at 5 feet 6 inches tall, was short and stocky and he put on a lot of weight. All the staff at the club, including the manager, tried to help him but David did not want to listen to their good advice. David is a good lad really but he liked a social life and did not really dedicate himself to being a professional footballer. I told him that he was going to blow his chances but I could not get my message through to him. Mind you, how could I if even Alex Ferguson had failed?

Eventually, everyone's patience ran out with him. David was given a free transfer and Bury signed him - with a little assistance from the Neville brothers. About this time David had just met his girlfriend and she really sorted him out. Sometimes that happens - as the proverb says, behind every good man is a good woman. Where all of us in football had been banging our heads against a brick wall, his girlfriend made him listen. David settled down, got himself fit and Bury Football Club must take a lot of credit, especially the then management-team Stan Ternent and Sam Ellis. Finally, he started doing justice to his ability and achieving what he should have done a lot earlier. From Gigg Lane he moved to Ipswich Town, where he blossomed under George Burley and helped the club gain promotion to the Premiership.

When I saw him last year, he told me that he now realised that he blew it at Manchester United. I said to him that he had obviously learned from his mistake and that he may be back with United in the future. They say in football that you should never go back to a club a second time. I do not agree because if you are good enough then why on earth not? Look at Stuart McCall, returning to Bradford City and helping them to get in and remain in the Premier League.

Serious injuries can be devastating for any player. Ben Thornley, who played in the same youth team as David Beckham and company, would have been playing in Manchester United's first team now but for a cruciate ligament injury. He was one of the best young wingers that I have ever worked with. Ben is now playing for Huddersfield Town and, with a little bit of luck, he will be back in the Premier League soon.

Michael Owen is a player that every club seemed to be after when he was at school. A few years ago, Manchester United took two teams to play at York; an under 15s team and an under 14s team. I looked after the under 15s, and Nobby Stiles took control of the younger lads. The two games were played on adjacent pitches and I kept glancing over to the other match because Michael was on that pitch. Believe you me I found it difficult to concentrate on my own game. I was craning my neck to look at the other game most of the time. At the end, Nobby came over to me and said, "We must try to sign young Owen because he has the potential to go all the way to the top." I fully agreed with Nobby, who was no mean judge of a player.

Before we left I spoke to Michael's parents, who were both at the tournament. They did not commit themselves when I asked them if they would bring Michael to the Cliff for some coaching. As we drove back to Manchester over the Pennines I thought that we were in with a chance but it was not to be.

Michael had his heart set on joining Liverpool. Steve Heighway, who I served with on the P.F.A. Working Party "A Kick in the Right Direction", about coaching and the professional game, and the rest of the coaching staff at Liverpool have done an excellent job in bringing Michael through to full international honours. I just wish that he had signed for United. Imagine Michael Owen, Dwight Yorke, Andy Cole and Teddy Sheringham linking up together!

The likes of Michael Owen and David Platt have driven themselves to the top because, yes they have been born with great natural talent, but also because, at a very early age, they mastered the basics of being a footballer.

When I am coaching young players, I constantly hammer home to them good basic principles. These are the correct training techniques for essentials like ball control, passing, crossing and shooting. For every youngster in Manchester United's youth team squad those techniques are part of their everyday routine for two years. They are drummed in with the emphasis on the fact that it is no good just shining at one of the skills. It is not much use controlling the ball if you then give it away. Similarly, you might be the greatest passer in the world but if you cannot control the ball in the first place you won't get the opportunity to show your passing skills.

If the youngsters apply themselves diligently and master the basics early on, the skills will remain with them for the rest of their lives. They are the foundation stones on which they can build their careers. It is like riding a bicycle - once learned, never forgotten.

It is not all about technique. To succeed at the very top of their profession, players require 100 per cent dedication and concentration, both in training and matches. They must also never be afraid to seek out advice if things are going wrong on the pitch. Any good coach will be only too pleased to help his players iron out any difficulties. A good coach is always interested. It is worth remembering the old adages, 'practice makes perfect' and 'if at first you do not succeed, try, try and try again.' Nothing comes easy in this life. If you do not believe me then ask one of Manchester United's biggest supporters, Geoffrey Boycott, how he made it to the top in cricket. Hard graft is the only route to the top - and then more hard graft is the only way to stay there.

When I was a young player, I was told never to let opponents see I was hurt. For instance, if the ball hit you in the private parts, you had to pretend that it did not hurt. I can tell you from personal experience that wasn't easy. It was difficult to control your body language when you got clattered - and bear in mind footballers were heavier during my playing career. Nevertheless, managers and trainers constantly told you that if an opponent kicked you, and it hurt, that you must disguise the pain. This was all done so your opponents could not win the psychological battle against you. Also they would not cause you further pain on an injured part of your anatomy. If someone was hobbling round trying to protect their left ankle, as sure as day follows night that ankle would be targeted by the next opponent's tackle. Ruthless game, football!

That has now changed in the modern game. Things have turned full circle. Some players, far from being determined to hide injuries, feign injury on a regular basis in games. Others can dive as well as Olympic champions. There is no disputing these facts. They are there for all spectators and television viewers to see. In the past there used to be a good healthy battle taking place on the field but now the poor referees are getting involved and have to decide whether a player is hurt or is he just feigning. Players do not like it when referees make on-the-spot wrong decisions but many of their actions do not help the referee to make the right judgement. Is it any good me telling my youngsters not to show that you are hurt? Would I be better telling them to feign injuries and to dive?

My answer remains constant. Never feign injuries and don't dive. Am I doing the right thing? After all, trying to con referees has been going on in Europe for decades. My conscience tells me that I am correct but there are those that disagree, believing tricks like that to be all part of the game.

A few years ago, a foreign coach visited United and watched all the teams at the club in both training and matches. I spoke to him quite often and one day was staggered to hear him suggest that I should teach players to dive. He honestly believed that there was no problem in teaching young players how to dive from an early age.

He reasoned that as most continental players used the 'tactic' - cheating, I call it - mainly to get a free-kick in an advantageous position, it was a useful skill to perfect. He never actually said that it was to get a player sent off as well, or at least to get him yellow-carded, but I am sure that he thought that. This is a big problem facing referees and I feel very sorry for them. What a thankless and difficult job they have got these days because winning at all costs is the order of the day and sportsmanship is rapidly declining.

I would like to see the PFA come out with a strong directive about feigning injury and diving. At the moment it is quite easy to get an opponent dismissed or yellow-carded which will guarantee him, or at least take him towards, a suspension which could cost prove very costly to his club. That sort of behaviour needs stamping out and with players apparently unwilling to stop it themselves the situation needs tough action from the top. We're still waiting.

11.

How Hoddle read Beckham all wrong

THE MOST IMPORTANT JOB of a youth coach is to develop players who are good enough to become members of the first team. To translate potential into achievement.

We are helping to turn boys into men and, without question, a young player with the correct attitude and preparation should get his chance in the first team early on.

A manager or coach has to have the courage of his convictions and confidence in his own judgment (it helps, of course, if his judgment is sound in the first place). Similar attributes are required when international managers face decisions on which players to elevate from club to country.

At club level, some managers are afraid to actually pick young players for the first team. Such a manager thinks that it is too risky and, instead, either sticks by his experienced players or will go out and buy an established player from another club - at the expense of the youngster's progress.

We are very lucky at Manchester United because, as I have said previously, the boss will always give a kid his chance. He knows that if a talented youngster is languishing in the reserves when he is worthy of a first-team place it will not only delay the player's progress but also make him unhappy and that's whan careers can go off-track. Also, there is the clear logic that a top quality young player will enhance the team anyway, given his chance.

For a youth coach to see the kids that he has developed play in the first team is a wonderful feeling. It is an experience that money just cannot buy and to see them playing internationals against the best players in the world is a dream. During my career I have been lucky enough to see a lot of young players who I have helped on their way, go on to play first-team football and then represent their countries.

When Alex Ferguson asked me if I would do some scouting at the 1998 World Cup in France, I jumped at the chance. I immediately thought of watching England and hopefully watching David Beckham, Gary Neville, Paul Scholes and Teddy Sheringham play in the competition. Naturally, I had a vested interest in the first three players because I had seen them develop from schoolboys to the top level in their careers.

The boss said that he wanted me to watch the group games in Nantes so I was disappointed to learn that England were not going to play there. Then I discovered that the England squad were training only about an hour's drive away from Nantes at La Baulle. I knew that La Baulle is a beautiful place, very close to the sea, and I decided that was the place where I was going to stay.

I told Gary Neville that I was going to stay at La Baulle and he suggested that I should visit the England training camp to watch the squad preparing for their matches. I said to him that it might be difficult for me to get inside the training camp, with all the security, so we left it at that.

I took Shirley, my youngest daughter Vicky and her boyfriend John to France. I made the trip a working holiday and needed my car to get to the games so Vicky and John shared the driving with me.

World Cups are always exciting and France '98 had an atmosphere as electric as any. The city of Nantes was buzzing with people

The View From the Dugout

and I found that the only way to get to the ground was by tram. I used to arrive in Nantes very early, have a coffee in the square and really soak up the atmosphere and entertainment. Many times I scratched my head, thinking how do football supporters afford to watch their beloved international teams? They poured in; Spaniards, Nigerians, Americans, Morroccans, Brazilians, Croatians, Japanese, Yugoslavians.

The colours, the costumes and the flags added to a carnival of colour. It was all quite breathtaking. The atmosphere and the excellent behaviour between the rival supporters was truly magnificent. I can honestly say that I did not see one bad incident. I saw football fans from many different countries talking together, laughing and drinking together at all times of day and night. Why can't it always be like that at football matches?

The tram ride to the stadium took about half an hour. Rival supporters were packed together like sardines but again there was no trouble. When America played Yugoslavia, trouble was forecast and I was a little nervous, mainly because I had taken my family with me, having been lucky enough to get three more tickets for the game from an American friend of mine. I need not have worried because both sets of supporters behaved impeccably.

On the tram to the game we were entertained for the whole journey by a Yugoslav-American who was not only very funny but very clever. When his mobile phone rang, he answered it and started talking in Yugoslavian in a very loud voice. All the Yugoslavs in the carriage were howling with laughter and we were laughing along with them, even though we could not understand a word. This went on for about ten minutes before he ended his call. About ten seconds later, his phone rang again and this time, speaking in English, he said: "Hello Mr President." He then went on entertaining all the Americans and the English and having them in stitches with his conversation. He was having us all believe that he was actually talking to President Clinton. One of the Yugoslavians who spoke English told me that before the call from Bill Clinton he was talking to the President of Yugoslavia. He was telling both presidents what he thought the teams would be and all kind of other rubbish but it was very funny indeed and the journey went very quickly.

That was an example of what the atmosphere of the World Cup was like. Personally, I enjoyed the four group games as much for the atmosphere and the lasting friendship as the games themselves.

I was walking through La Baulle two days before England's first game against Tunisia when I bumped into an old acquaintance. He worked for Carling and I had spoken to him a few times before. He suggested that I should pop round to his hotel where he was staying, along with most of the English reporters. He told me that Joe Melling and Bob Cass, who worked for the Mail on Sunday, were staying there.

Joe and Bob are old friends of mine and I did not hesitate to go round. They are two of the funniest men that I have ever met so I knew that I would be in for some fun. The laughter came later in the week when I had a few nights out with them.

It's very nice to have friends in the media that you can talk to in confidence, without fear of being quoted. Nevertheless, they were both a bit solemn when they told me that David Beckham and Gary Neville were not going to be chosen for the first game against Tunisia. Bob and Joe knew that I would be upset to hear the news and they were perfectly correct of course.

They also told me that Glenn Hoddle, the England manager, had said that he did not think that David Beckham was focussed enough for the game and I was staggered beyond belief. We were talking about a boy who had practiced from morning until night, day in and day out, throughout his career. A boy who had sacrificed so much during his short life and I could not believe that anybody could ever accuse him of not being focussed. Coming from Hoddle, who was one of England's most skilful footballers, it was truly amazing. In fact, I thought that it was an insult. The World Cup has got to be the most important aspect in any footballer's life. How could Hoddle say David was not focussed for something for which he had been waiting for years?

Naturally, knowing how disappointed they would be, I wanted to speak to the players as quickly as possible. I got through on the phone at the England headquarters and spoke to Gary first. He was not too bad because he thought that he might still have a chance of playing because Gareth Southgate had a bit of an injury.

I then spoke to David and, as I thought, he was obviously upset. I told him to remain positive and to remember all the practicing which he had done in his life, preparing him for occasions like the World Cup. I emphasised to David that in my opinion he was totally focussed. Hoddle was wrong and would be proved wrong. I told David that he was a great player and he must remember that - today, tomorrow and at all times.

Hoddle could not keep him out of the England team, I added, and when he brought David back into the team he would score his first goal for England. I remained very positive throughout the conversation and I expected him to react with typical strength of character and to start thinking positive. Negative thoughts are no good to any sportsperson. Sure enough, David came on as a substitute against Columbia and scored his first goal for England. I must either be a good judge or a lucky man.

To see Gary Neville, Paul Scholes and David Beckham playing together for England in the World Cup brought a lump to my throat - and me a dour Yorkshireman. It was the most wonderful of feelings to see my former charges playing at the top level and entertaining millions of people throughout the world. Football, though, is full of highs and lows and sometimes they follow each other very quickly. My working holiday was going absolutely brilliantly - then came the England game against Argentina.

Finally, I managed to make a visit to England's training camp and when I did I received two shocks. A middle-aged couple started talking to me outside the training camp - they were in France to watch the group games at Nantes - and to my amazement they started bragging about selling two of their tickets. They said that they were shopping in Nantes when a Japanese man approached them and asked them if they had any tickets for the Japan v Croatia game. They replied that they had two and the Japanese guy offered them £600 for the pair. They sold the tickets and proceeded to tell me that the transaction had virtually paid for their holiday.

Apparently, Japan received an allocation of 5,000 for the game against Croatia. I think there were 25,000 Japanese supporters at the match, which meant that 20,000 tickets had been bought on the black market. That staggered me but I should not have been surprised because every game I went to at Nantes, there were touts openly selling tickets. In fact, I saw two American touts at the four games which I attended with a wadful of tickets. How can these people operate in this day and age? Where do they get these tickets from? Surely in a technological era the authorities could stop this sort of thing happening?

The other shock that I got was the rigid security when I visited England's training headquarters. Gaining entry into Fort Knox would be a piece of cake in comparison. The difference between the English and, say, the Norwegian approach was total. For example, the Norwegian wives and girlfriends were staying at the same apartment block as myself and my family and, after training, the Norwegian players visited the girls and soaked up a bit of sun, had a swim and generally relaxed with their loved ones.

I asked Ole Solskjar if I could watch the Norwegian players training and he said yes, no problem. I am not convinced that the Norwegian approach was better than the English approach but I was surprised that there was such a massive difference in preparation methods.

I had to wait an age before I got inside the England headquarters. I tried to tell the gendarme that I had an official invitation but my approach fell on deaf ears. Finally, a gentleman from the Football Association came along and said that Hoddle's assistant, John Gorman, had instructed him to let me in. I was very grateful to John for allowing me to watch the training session. I love watching top class players going through their work routines and I certainly was not disappointed on this occasion. The session that I watched was first-class.

It was just like watching a club team in action. You can always sense when team-spirit among a group of players is as buoyant as it should be and that was the case here. I was very impressed and I was getting more excited by the minute. I began to think to myself that we could win the World Cup. John Gorman, who I had known for a number of years, came over to me and we had a chat. I thought that it was very nice of him to take time. Peter Taylor (another one of Hoddle's staff and now doing such a fine job as Leicester) also joined us and I told both of them how impressed I was by the standard of the training. I have a very high regard for Peter, who was, of course, sacked as manager of England under 21s despite having built a fantastic record at that level. Everyone who I have spoken to who has worked with Peter Taylor agrees that he is an excellent coach and a first-class man. For England to sack him and then later instal him as caretaker manager of the senior team was absolutely amazing. If that had been me I would have told the FA where to stick their offer. The FA never cease to amaze me.

Back to that England World Cup camp, the player who impressed me most of all was Michael Owen. He was scoring goals like shelling peas and he was scoring them against a top class goalkeeper in David Seaman. Owen went through his full repertoire. He smashed the ball into the net, bent the ball into the net, side-footed the ball into the net, chipped the ball into the net. He dribbled the ball past the diving Seaman and put the ball into the far corner. It was a wonderful exhibition of goal-scoring. Owen, with luck, will be one of the all-time greats.

I went away from the training camp feeling very confident about England's chances in the World Cup and slept very soundly that night.

I watched the England and Argentina match in a bar in La Baulle. The atmosphere in that bar was electric and when the incident with Beckham and Simone happened there was almost total silence. The bar was full of a mixture of English and French and before the game started some of the French people told me that they wanted England to win and quite naturally some of them said that they wanted Argentina to win.

No-one could believe what was happening. It was slow-motion stuff. Simone seemed to be on the ground for ages before Beckham flicked out his foot at him. It then seemed an eternity before the referee showed Beckham the red card. From that moment on, as I watched David trudging off the field looking as stunned as we all felt, my working holiday went from brilliant to depressing. I could not wait to return home.

In every corner of England, it seemed that everybody was talking about the World Cup before, during and after. In fact after the World Cup, it seemed that every single person was in a debating mood. I think that debate is the correct word. Could we have won it, should we have won it if Beckham had stayed on the pitch?

The nation was getting hot under the collar. I was defending David Beckham and I got involved in some very nasty arguments with normally placid people who I knew were letting rip and taking their frustrations out on me because I knew David. These were the same people who had previously said to me for years that football is only a game. That mentality was abandoned during and after the World Cup. Nevertheless, I stuck to my convictions that David Beckham would grow in stature and become a world class player.

Kevin Keegan said at the 2000 European Championship that, despite the abuse which Beckham has to suffer, he has no problem with the player's temperament - and he has the ability to become a great international player. Keegan was right. Hoddle was sadly wrong.

Beckham has justified all my faith in him and bounced back to the top in international competitions with consistent impressive displays. He should captain his country for years to come.

Meanwhile, many people are still criticising Phil Neville for England's exit from Euro 2000 after conceding the late penalty to Romania but at 23 years of age, he will mature. He will learn from his mistakes and become an established England international alongside Beckham. Their manager, Sir Alex Ferguson, would never allow such natural talent to be wasted.

12.

Will England ever win the World Cup again?

ONE OF THE QUESTIONS I am most often asked is will England ever win the World Cup again?

We will not be hosting the tournament again for a long time so will not be able to enjoy the unquestionable advantage of being roared on as the host nation. That means that if we are to reclaim the world's premier football trophy in the short or medium term it will be on foreign soil. And that means, as I think was proven by our disappointing performances in Euro 2000, that we must continue to improve technically.

The roots have been put down. There is more coaching going on now for youngsters at professional football clubs than ever before. More money than ever is being channelled into youth development. Forty clubs in the English Premiership and Football League now run their own Football Academies. The top man in charge of these organisations is Howard Wilkinson, who has vast experience at all levels in the game and, of course, steered Leeds United to the Premiership title in 1992. He is now the Football Association's technical director.

The View From the Dugout

The objective of the academies is to produce world class players for their clubs; players who will in turn enhance England's chances of winning the World Cup. In theory, the idea looks very good but now we have to be fully committed, at all levels, to putting it into practice.

Today's young players are receiving more coaching than any in the history of the game. The facilities are better than ever and still improving. The question is, will this compensate for the lack of individual practicing?

This aspect concerns me because I hardly ever seem to see kids kicking a ball against a wall these days. That was standard practice years ago but, driving around the country, I never seem to see kids practicing in the streets. To see boys kicking and heading a ball around in every available space was the commonest of occurrence years ago. Nowadays I never see kids practice with a tennis ball - and I don't mean for playing tennis at Wimbledon. There are so many other leisure pursuits available to youngsters now, of course, like computers and the internet. I could go on and on about individual practice which is so essential if players are going to reach international level.

Practice makes perfect in any sport. Just ask David Beckham. Or Geoff Boycott. Or Steve Redgrave. Or Naseem Hamed. Or Stephen Hendry. Any great sportsman. They have all reached the top of their respective trees by putting in the practice. Hour after hour. Day after day. Year after year.

Another factor is that youth coaches, by and large, are doing good jobs for their clubs but how long will they stay as youth coaches? There is a different sort of pressure on them, these days, with more and more money from TV coverage flooding into the game. Will these youth coaches be content to work with the youngsters or want to step up the proverbial ladder and go for more money and fame in the realms of management? Can their egos allow them to remain youth coaches for the rest of their careers? To be called assistant manager or the boss certainly sounds far more glamorous.

I am encouraged by the fact that more and more clubs are now recognising the value of youth coaches. More youth set-ups are getting funding which, historically, they have always had to fight and beg for. The realisation is sinking in that clubs which keep changing their youth coaches will fail. Chairmen and managers now appreciate that clubs require continuity at the grass roots level. There is a saying in football that the most important coach is the first one the boys deal with - the one who sets out the ground-rules to make good footballers. Without stability at that level, a club will flounder because its foundation is not solid.

When the youth policy is not producing the goods, questions need to be asked. For instance, is it the club's fault or is it the coach's fault? Perhaps a combination of the two factors. Should the youth coach be paid more? If the youth coach is well paid, he is more likely to be motivated and wish to remain in his coaching position.

When I was youth coach at Everton and I was promoted to the reserve team coach and then first team coach under Gordon Lee I was so excited that I had no hesitation in accepting the jobs. At that time I was young and inexperienced and with a young family I suppose that I was looking after number one. Looking back I feel I would have derived much more satisfaction from sticking with the youngsters and working with them to try to set up a conveyor belt of talent into the senior sides.

If we are going to produce world class youngsters who are going to help England win the World Cup again, we must have continuity at youth level at our clubs. Any professional football club that has a good youth coach should make sure he stays because he will repay them four-fold by producing home grown footballers for the first team squad. However, if the youth coach is not good enough the club must get rid of him very quickly because he may be teaching youngsters bad habits which will impede their progress in the game. A good coach is invaluable. A bad coach is a nuisance.

The View From the Dugout

The other bee that I have in my bonnet is what happens when the young players get into the first team. For young footballers, the Premiership and the Football League are like assault courses. There are too many games which entail too much travelling. There are too many international matches and not enough time to prepare for games. The list just goes on and on. What about the young players in the team who we are expecting to become world class players? Do they now just get by through experience? Don't we have enough time to coach them anymore?

If England maintains its continuity at youth level - and young first-team players continue to receive quality coaching - we will produce world class players. That way, we can win the World Cup again during my lifetime. There can be no greater incentive than to help your country to lift that ultimate of trophies - the Jules Rimet. The powers that be who run football know that for England to regain the World Cup would do the sport in this country more good, in terms of the future, than all the other initiatives, however worthy, put together. Our players have the ability - we just need to equip them with sufficently highly-skilled coaches. If everyone pulls in the same direction the World Cup will be back in English hands in the not-too-distant future.

13.

The folly of "long ball"

IN RECENT YEARS, the Football Association has made increasingly strenuous efforts to ensure that the coaches attending their coaching schemes are groomed in the correct way. The trouble is they are still making up for the years when Charles Hughes was the director of coaching.

Then, the principles of play being taught were abysmal. Youngsters' heads were filled with bad advice and both our national team and domestic football has been battling to break free of those chains ever since. English football is now winning its race to match the best countries in the world in terms of technique but that has begun to happen only since coaches and players "unlearned" what they were told during the dreadful years under Hughes' control. In the quest for football credibility, they were wasted years.

The dreaded POMO - the Position of Maximum Opportunity - was being rammed down every coach's throat on every conceivable occasion. What that really meant was long balls constantly fired upfield, generally bypassing the midfield players. The midfielders, who were often the most skilful players in the team, then had to sprint forward as fast as they could to support the strikers. Players who were competent at passing and dribbling were ordered to spend their time chasing and harrying. Ninety-five per cent of their effort and energy was expended without the ball at their feet. It was like asking Leonardo Da Vinci to paint garage doors.

Usually the long balls were played into the corner of the pitch, obviously in the opponents half, hoping that a corner or a throw-in would result. The theory was that the closer you were to the opponents' goal, the greater the chance of the ball ending up in that goal, but of course this was deeply flawed logic. The more the tactic was employed without variation - and there was never a Plan B - the more comfortable the opposition's defence became with it.

Charles Hughes and, it appeared, his staff coaches were adamant that the POMO strategy was the only way forward. Most frighteningly, that gospel was being preached to coaches at English football's coaching control centre, Lilleshall. The finest and most promising coaches were assembled and then their heads filled with absolute garbage. It was staggeringly self-defeating.

It soon became obvious that a lot of managers and coaches had taken the theory on board because many club sides were playing in that fashion. Some, like Wimbledon, Watford and Cambridge United, were actually achieving success using it.

Charles Hughes even went on record to say that if Brazil ever played that way, every other country in the world would be in great trouble! Unbelievable. Brazil, who thrill almost every football supporter in the world, reduced to that long-ball rubbish? I'm sure they would rather take up cricket.

Jim Smith, now manager of Derby County and approaching his fourth decade in League management, expressed serious doubts about Charles Hughes's theories from the outset. Jim never utilised the POMO method and yet has tasted more than his fair share of success and survived to become one of the longest-serving Premier League managers.

During the Hughes era managers and coaches throughout the world were constantly laughing at English football. This great game of ours was being held back. Top journalists like Brian Glanville were constantly writing about it and complaining bitterly in the national newspapers. What did the mandarins do at the Football Association? Despite poor international results, they just buried their heads in the sand.

For me it was just like playing in the lower divisions but this magic formula was supposed to cover a multitude of sins and become the redemption of English football. I thought to myself, how will defenders ever learn to pass the ball into midfield? How will midfield players learn to receive the ball from a defender? And how are forwards ever going to learn to receive a ball into their feet if they are always chasing long balls. Did the Hughes regime want to turn footballers into workhorses?

I honestly don't think that any of the coaches employed by the Football Association at this time understood the importance and value of possession football. Quite simply, your opponents cannot play without the ball. I don't think that those in charge realised how soul-destroying it is for opponents when a team is keeping hold of the ball for long periods of time throughout the game.

They did not appear to understand how players could lose concentration or be dragged out of position by teams who passed the ball well and moved after they had passed it. That is what the Football Association should have been teaching our professional coaches at Lilleshall in that delightful part of Shropshire. Not the POMO drivel which never brought the results the sages at Lancaster Gate promised.

In despair, I stopped attending the coaching courses at Lilleshall in the late 1980s along with many others. I had formulated my own ideas and they were the absolute opposite to most of the nonsense generated by Hughes and Co.

The coaching scheme is much better now so I am more optimistic for the future. I would be even more optimistic if the Professional Footballers Association could take over the running of all the coaching schemes in the country.

I sat on a working party, run by the Professional Footballers Association in 1994. Our brief was to come up with some ideas on how to improve the skills of young players, especially those who had an international future, so the home countries could benefit and match the rest of the world.

The panel was chaired by Paul Power, the former Manchester City and Everton player, who at the time was working with the PFA. He is now the youth development officer at Manchester City and doing an excellent job at Maine Road. Also on the panel, brought together from the PFA committee headed by the popular and knowledgeable chief executive of the players' union, Gordon Taylor, were Don Howe, Steve Heighway, John Cartwright, Jimmy Armfield (as an observer), Mick Wadsworth, now with Bobby Robson at Newcastle, Howard Kendall and Micky Burns (education Officer at the PFA). Views were also sought, on a consultation basis, from other coaches of high quality. These included former Manchester United and Coventry City manager Dave Sexton, Terry Venables, later to become England manager, and Graham Taylor, who also aspired to the same role. Bobby Robson, architect of all that stylishly-achieved success at Ipswich, was also consulted, as were Andy Roxburgh, who is now technical director at UEFA, and Gerard Houllier, now known to us all as Liverpool's manager. It was a highly impressive list of talented people who have reached the top of their profession and I felt very honoured to be involved with them.

The first meeting was very informal and we just threw ideas about like a brainstorming session. The first idea that I threw at the rest of the panel was that how could we expect to produce world-class youngsters if the coaching was not up to scratch. I suggested that the PFA ran the coaching schemes in Great Britain and I visualised the staff coaches being made up of former players who had developed as coaches, had the right habits instilled in them and would pass them on. In this way those good habits would be perpetuated from one generation to the next and each generation would encourage players to play the game in the correct way. As Brian Clough always insisted, on the ground.

I still firmly believe that this is the way forward - for the PFA to pull the coaching strings - but I don't hold out much hope of it happening. It would mean the Football Association relinquishing some of their power and they are always loathe to do that.

Currently, there are four organisations running football; the FA, the Football League, the Premier League and the PFA. If they all amalgamated into one cohesive unit there would be less fragmentation and self-preservation. It all comes back round to the idea of all pulling in the same direction. If people pull in different ways, everyone's progress is hampered.

The idea of amalgamation was put forward by Sir Robert Atkins when he was the Minister for Sport. I fully endorsed his suggestion at the time and still do, but I can't see it happening. Too many people want to protect their own power-bases. The greater good - the good of the game - is, to them, secondary.

Sir Alex Ferguson has urged England to axe international friendlies. He said: "Eventually they will have to stop England friendly games because there are going to be more European club matches. It's an abortive exercise because there are so many competitive games now and you never get a full team."

For instance, how often can you remember any British international manager being able to field his strongest side from the squad originally chosen? The last thing Fergie wants is his exhausted stars hauled off to different parts of the world in the close-season for meaningless fixtures. He reckons that self-interest is clouding the issue and accuses football's boardroom personnel of failing to think of the players.

I agree with all Sir Alex's statements because if international players such as David Beckham, Paul Scholes and Michael Owen, and many others in the home international squads, are not given more rest then they could face physical burn-out and be lost to the game prematurely.

The solution, in my opinion, is to scrap international friendlies but demand that all players called up by their countries attend training camps when there is a break in the league programmes. To achieve any success at international level, especially for the smaller nations - like us at Wales - getting players together to work on team play is vital and bringing players together for training camps, without the fear of sustaining injury, should be acceptable to club managers. FIFA rules state that league clubs must release players for up to seven friendly matches a year but everybody knows this is not put into practice. That leads to a big problem for any player who wants to be released for friendlies but finds his manager opposed to the idea. The player then has the worry that the manager might have it in for him when he gets back from international duty. That is a difficult situation for players and most opt out, knowing where their bread and butter comes from. Replacing friendly matches with training camps, which are invaluable for team-building but do not carry the risk of injury, seems to me the ideal solution. If club managers don't accept that then I don't think anything will keep them happy.

There are financial considerations as well, of course. If countries can make a lot of money out of friendlies then that is another matter because a lot of the less affluent countries badly need the cash. Those for whom money is not a problem, however, should play either very few friendlies or none at all.

14.

The Dark Ages

CHARLES HUGHES KEPT ENGLISH FOOTBALL in the dark ages. His long ball tactics would have ruined the game if every manager and coach had gone along with them.

Coaches can be brainwashed and a lot of brainwashing was going on during his reign. I believe coaches must use their imagination and not be slaves to a formula. Under his supervision there was no scope for imagination or improvisation from coaches or players. Taking it to the most ludicrous extreme, players have even been substituted on the spot for doing something that went against the letter of the team plan. Surely, it is skilled players, with imagination and initiative, that we want to cultivate, not robots.

One area where we are definitely not as good as the foreign players is the art of receiving the ball. Charles Hughes' reign widened the gap between our players and those abroad who receive possession immaculately, a skill which, in turn, makes it to so much easier to distribute the next pass. The more seconds it takes to bring the ball under control, the greater time it gives an opponent to arrive to put your next move under pressure.

Under Hughes, goalkeepers, defenders and midfielders were all instructed - I won't say coached because you hardly need coaching to boot the ball upfield - to hit long balls into corners of the pitch. There the forwards, invariably hemmed in by defenders, were expected to work some kind of magic or, much more likely, belt the ball against a defender to obtain a corner-kick or a throw-in. Long throws were developed and, along with corners, became the principal scoring threat. Open play was targeted, not at getting the ball into the goal but forcing a set-piece, the theory being that a lot of goals were scored from set-pieces. That is true, but what about the overall development of our players? What happens when, as was inevitable, the predictable tactic was worked out and comfortably dealt with? What then? Where was the quality going to come from?

There was a school of thought that Charles Hughes had borrowed ideas from a retired RAF officer called Charles Reep. In the 1950s Reep, apparently, had worked on something called Match Analysis which purported to show that the most effective form of football - and the greatest number of goals - came from the use of the long pass. Brazil, it was suggested, had got it wrong. It seems hard to believe, now, that such preposterous rubbish was given any time at all but, sadly, it found some disciples. And those disciples passed it on to - poor souls - the young players at their clubs.

A deeply worrying situation was that England's youth team was employing these tactics. In the early 1980s, I reprimanded my youth team goalkeeper, a boy called Fraser Digby who went on to have an excellent career and is still playing professional football, for kicking every single ball out of his hands, high, long, and not so handsome. He was playing for England's youth team at the time but I still had a go at him when he got back to Manchester. I forbade him to do that when he was playing for our youth team. In fact he hardly ever kicked the ball out of his hands for us. He usually rolled the ball out to one of his defenders, which meant that we kept possession and could build rather than hoping to salvage the ball from a heading duel from a hoof upfield. His answer was that he had been told to boot the ball up the field for England. What enlightened instruction from a national coach!

How were defenders going to learn to be comfortable with the ball at their feet with that kind of coaching going on? How were the midfield players going to learn the art of ball-control? How were the forwards going to learn to receive the ball to their feet when they spent most of their time running into the corners of the pitch? How were teams going to learn how to keep possession of the ball? The opposition can't score when your team is in possesion, and believe me, it is horrible playing against a team which can keep the ball for long periods. That is when concentration goes and when that happens the skill-level drops when you do finally get the ball.

How do you learn to slow the game down, and speed it up, if you can't keep possession? How do you play abroad when the temperature is in the eighties or nineties and you need to keep the ball and build slowly? Where will the power-play get you then?

While all this poor coaching was going on at our courses - remember the coaches, not just the players, were being told to do this - the coaching abroad was carrying on as usual. There they were teaching the young players the correct footballing habits, learning how to receive the ball and teaching the players that before you receive you look over your shoulder to see if there is an opposing player close to you. If a player does that, he knows what he is going to do with the ball before it comes to him. Simple isn't it? Next time you watch a football match at any level, see which player looks before he receives a ball. You will be amazed how many players don't!

The coaches abroad were teaching players how to dribble but also showing them how to get into position, before they got the ball, to be in a position to dribble. To find space. Think about the Brazilians and the Dutch. While these kind of habits were drummed into their players, ours were being ordered to boot the ball up field. They were cultivating pedigree animals. We were rearing headless chickens. Quite a difference.

The inflexibility of the the FA coaching scheme - and one of the reasons why it was destined for failure - was perfectly illustrated by an incident when I attended a refresher course in the 1970s. The first session of the week was conducted by an FA staff coach and revolved around his strikers. The object of his exercise was for the defenders to play the ball up the side of the pitch for the strikers to gain possession. The players involved were all coaches attending the course and I was playing centre-back, defending against the striker who was supposed to get the ball before me. My experience told me to get to the ball before the striker and this I did, much to the annoyance of the staff coach. After three or four attempts, the coach angrily called a halt and accused me of ruining his session, saying that I would not defend that way if this was a league match. My answer to him was that I did it for 17 years as a pro. If he had used his imagination, he would have instructed the defender to play the ball away from where I was standing and let the striker get to the ball. No chance. Deviation from the Big Brother plan was not allowed and, knowing exactly what was coming, I could have cleared the ball all day.

It did not finish there. All the coaches had to do two coaching sessions that week and the staff coach decided what topic we were getting. As punishment for having had the temerity to expose the earlier session as a sham, my two topics both revolved around goalkeeping (hardly my specialist subject). The first was dealing with high crosses, the second was diving at a forward's feet. My first demonstration was catching a high cross and one of my friends on the course was a lad called Charlie Wright, who was a goalkeeper at Bolton. He was playing as a striker against me and as I went for the first cross, he knocked the daylights out of me and dumped me in the mud - it had been raining all week. He laughed at me and said that's what goalkeepers have to put up with. I had a good laugh with Charlie and I made my two sessions into two very light-hearted sessions, thinking how pathetic it was that I was being punished for defending well during the staff coach's session. The whole experience helped convince me that under that regime England had about as much chance of winning the World Cup as dear old Halifax Town had of winning the European Cup.

15.

Jealousy and friendship

MANY RIVAL SUPPORTERS around the country and the world detest Manchester United. Some of their hostility appears to run so deep as to be pure hatred but the principal cause is, of course, jealously. For every club, it seems, it is the highlight of the season if their team can beat Manchester United.

I have personally been on the receiving end of this frenzied hate on a few occasions. One of these incidents absolutely staggered me - a Yorkshireman - in my the county of my birth at Leeds United.

The relationship between some sections of the two club's supporters had taken an ugly turn and feelings were running high when Manchester United played a League Cup semi-final at Elland Road in 1992. During the match I sat right at the end of the bench inside the dug-out and when Lee Sharpe scored for us, I jumped up with excitement like the rest of our bench. Out of the corner of my eye, I saw a figure coming quickly towards me and I soon realised it was a very large figure. A Leeds supporter had jumped out of the crowd and, having avoided detection, made a beeline for me. He punched me square on the jaw and I went down, shocked as well as hurt, like a sack of spuds.

Steve Bruce, who must have been injured that day because I

can rarely remember him being dropped from the first team, was standing next to me. He did not know whether to pick me up off the ground or try to grab the offender. Amid all the confusion, my assailant had quickly jumped back into the crowd without the police or stewards apprehending him.

Steve was very concerned about my welfare and asked me if I required some medical attention. I replied that I was fine, even though this thug had landed me with a real haymaker of a punch which left me battered and bruised for a few days.

Never being one to let the opposition know that I was hurt, I said to Steve that I could understand that the Leeds supporters would be sick that we had scored. That young man had gone too far though in venting his frustration on me. Steve suggested that I had probably been a victim of mistaken identity. I do look a bit like Alex Ferguson and the Leeds fan probably thought that he was going to get himself on all the front pages by decking the top man. He was disappointed but at least had the satisfaction of getting away. The Boss got away unscathed, of course, while I was the one who ended up with a three-day headache.

Alex, in his book, "Managing my life," referred to the incident and suggested how noble it was of me to draw fire that was meant for him. He ended by stating: "Well done, Eric, such self-sacrifice does not go unnoticed." Anyway, once we got inside the safety of the dressing room, I said to the boss, friendship or no friendship that was the last time that I was going to take a right-hander for him.

We had a good laugh about it but he was seriously concerned about the unsavoury incident. Some of the directors and their wives had had drink thrown over them that night but we all kept quiet about the incidents. I certainly did not want my incident to become public knowledge so that was it as far as I was concerned. If the incidents had been reported, the Leeds supporters would have got their club into trouble with the authorities. Great rivals though we are, we would not want Leeds to suffer because of a few mindless supporters.

What many supporters do not understand is the amount of friendship which exists between rival football clubs. After the game, which we won 1-0, the Leeds manager Howard Wilkinson and his backroom staff invited Alex Ferguson and his staff for a drink and some light refreshments. This is something which happens at most clubs once the referee has blown the final whistle and the press conferences (which are these days insisted upon by the FA Carling Premiership) have finished.

So while some rival fans were outside in the cold, trying to scratch each other's eyes out, both sets of club officials were having a drink together, and guess what they were talking about - football.

Howard Wilkinson was the last to arrive. He was obviously upset at losing but the look on his face made it clear that something else was bothering him. He told us that the referee was going to report Leeds United because someone in the crowd had thrown a coin at the linesman. He continued: "It's bad enough losing to you lot but now we have got this to contend with."

I smiled to myself and looked at Alex Ferguson. We knew that Leeds United would be in deep trouble if I opened my mouth.

The friendship of the two sides continued off the field and a few years later Paul Hart, who was the Leeds United youth team manager, came over to see me at the Cliff, with the approval of Howard Wilkinson and Alex Ferguson.

He asked me how we had brought the young players through at Old Trafford to the first team. We sat and talked for a couple of hours and I helped the young man all I could. Our conversation obviously did no harm because Paul, who incidentally was a very good central defender, has been instrumental in developing some of the outstanding young players who are now making Leeds United a very exciting team - and a very strong adversary for us, which is good for the Premier League.

A lot of supporters will probably think that my prolonged

chat with Paul Hart was unusual and illogical - maybe even bordering on treachery! But that's the way it is in football. It is a huge industry with a lot of people happy to spend time helping each other out - even if they are from other, even rival, clubs. How I loved my chats with the legendary Bill Shankly - a Liverpool legend helping out an Everton coach! Football can be a cut-throat, dog-eat-dog business but also one with a lot of warmth and kindness and long may it remain so in the beautiful game.

Following his dismissal as Leeds United manager, Howard Wilkinson became the FA's technical director and played an integral part in the setting up of football academies throughout the country. As millions of pounds have been poured into youth football there is as much responsibility on Howard Wilkinson as Sven Goran Eriksson for England to become a top international team. One repercussion from England's Euro 2000 debacle may be an increasing influence of Howard Wilkinson's technical department at Lancaster Gate. Managers will come and go but Wilkinson's department has an infrastructure and long-term formula in place.

Manchester United have enjoyed sustained success at the top level throughout the world because all their teams, at all age-levels, have played the same system. That makes it easier for players to move through the different levels to the top flight. All the coaches are employing the same methods.

Now Howard Wilkinson has every England team from under 16s upwards under his command. They all play the same formation that research shows offers the best opportunity of learning how to be successful in international football. This system, together with monitoring how countries like Holland, France and Portugal operate, is supposed to be the best way forward for English football. I only hope that Sven Goran Eriksson and Howard Wilkinson are singing from the same hymn-sheet.

16.

Unsung heroes; the scouts

YOUNG PLAYERS JOIN the youth system at Manchester United in a multitude of ways. For instance, local schoolboys, whom I still coach two evenings a week, are brought into the club on the recommendations of our scouts. Periodically, trial games are held at the Cliff when youngsters from throughout the United Kingdom are put through their paces. The best ones are asked to return in their school holidays. Those who then impress again progress into the B Team and subsequently into the youth team. Of course, the drop-out rate is high - competition is fierce as only the very best will make the grade.

One thing that all youngsters must remember when signing for a club is that only they can ultimately drive themselves up into a first-team place. Nobody else can do it for them. Of course, good coaching and management helps but whatever they produce when they get onto the football field determines how far they can progress in their chosen career.

The proven way of providing the raw materials - talented but unpolished footballers - for clubs is from trusted scouts. Some of these people are former players. Others have run junior football clubs. Manchester United have 32 scouts operating throughout Great

Britain and Ireland. They receive an annual retainer plus additional bonus payments when a boy signs for the club, again when he signs apprentice forms, then when he signs as a professional, and finally when he has played a specified number of games for the first team. There is also an additional payment if he represents his country.

The schoolboy training and trials are still conducted at the Cliff but the majority of youth training and coaching is carried out at our new training ground at Carrington. This is a green field site, unlike the Cliff, of over 100 acres combined with state-of-the-art facilities which include physiotherapy, podiatry, dietetics, nutrition and swimming pool with a jacuzzi.

It is all completely different from my playing days, as so it should be. In the 1960s, basically you were just taken on as an apprentice with maybe a few words of advice from the manager and perhaps one or two older pros and then it was a case of sink or swim. Now we know that approach will waste an awful lot of talent, especially as these days there are so many other pursuits for young men to follow.

Young talent must be nurtured properly. Our FA Youth Cup record at Old Trafford suggests we are doing it correctly. My teams appeared in five finals and won two although my record pales into insignificance compared with the legendary Busby Babes who won five FA Youth Cup finals. I think the late Sir Matt's record will be difficult to beat because the competition from opponents is much tougher now with much more emphasis on youth team football at professional clubs. Most of them have their own academies with qualified coaches from an early age coaching schoolboys.

Obviously home-grown talent is the much preferred route because it saves clubs money in the long-run but periodically you have to buy to strengthen your squad. For example, Lee Sharpe was signed by Manchester United from Torquay United for £180,000. He was a product of Torquay's youth training scheme, turned out to be a good buy and progressed to the first team. Lee scored the only goal in the League Cup semi-final at Elland Road against Leeds United (a goal which I have special reason to remember, of course, as one Leeds fan decided to practice his right-hook on me). Lee also made eight appearances for England while he was at Old Trafford, between 1991 and 1994, and certainly represented value for money. Ironically, he joined Leeds United from Manchester United and consequently helped Bradford City retain their place in the Premier League after their initial season in the top flight.

One of the finest scouts employed by Manchester United until his death was Billy Behan. One of the players Billy brought into the club was Kevin Moran, who subsequently went on to play 69 times for the Republic of Ireland and, less happily, become the first player ever to be sent off in an FA Cup Final at Wembley. Thankfully this did not affect his career and the experience, although traumatic at the time, probably made him more determined than ever to succeed at the very top of his profession. Another good scout who I have worked with is Eddie Coulter, who introduced Keith Gillespie to me and the club.

It is invidious, though, to pick out individual scouts because all our scouts are of a high quality and utterly dedicated to football and Manchester United. These hardy souls stand out in all weathers to see junior games with little or no shelter in the depth of winter. Our chief scout, Les Kershaw, is a font of all knowledge and an excellent administrator. Perhaps these skills stemmed from his academic background as a university lecturer.

I still scout for the club most Saturdays unless I am employed on other matters with Wales. With matches now taking place on most days or evenings this can mean covering three or four games a week. In this role I can be looking at future first-team opposition and preparing a dossier for the manager on strengths and weaknesses of the forthcoming opponents. My other mission, on occasions, is looking at players in lower divisions and assessing their potential. In that capacity, I sometimes use friends who have a wealth of football experience such as Colin Appleton.

Scouting is a frustrating job really because 95% of the time you look at a player and realise that he could never get into our first team. It can also be frustrating because you might fancy a player who is not available or you may like a player but Alex Ferguson does not rate him.

Scouting goes on every week, virtually every day. We look at players who we think could play in our reserves and could eventually develop into first team players but that does not happen very often. We would rather groom our own kids. Sir Alex will give a young player a chance in the first team. That is one of the great rewards for the coaches at United. It must be heartbreaking to coach young players and have belief in them but secretly suspect that they will never be given the opportunity to play in the first team. It must be even worse for the players. We are extremely lucky at Old Trafford that our manager gives the youngsters the opportunity.

One thing I really love about scouting is going round to different grounds every week. It does not matter to me whether it is Halifax Town or Liverpool, the hospitality is usually great. Manchester City, our great rivals, are wonderful hosts.

Three years ago, I went up to watch Newcastle United play on a horrible night, freezing with snow coming down. The car park attendant, realising I had driven a long way on such a wretched night, ushered me to the best parking space in the ground. That is what I call a good club.

The vast majority of clubs and people at them are wonderful but you do come across the very occasional exception. I wrote in an earlier chapter of an unsavoury experience at the hands of a Leeds United supporter at Elland Road. On another occasion, England were playing Sweden, also at Elland Road as it happened. Brian Kidd had two tickets for the match but at the last minute he could not go so he asked me to go instead. It was an official scouting mission so I said yes.

The View From the Dugout

I asked a pal of mine if he wanted to come along and he said yes and said he would drive me to Leeds. We had a car-park pass to collect so we drove to the main entrance where the commissionaire stopped the car and asked us who we were. I explained that Brian Kidd could not come and I had taken his place and that I was wanting to pick up my car-park pass and my two match tickets. The commisionaire was making sure I was not trying to con him so I had to explain that I was the youth team manager at Manchester United. All of a sudden, when the name Manchester United was mentioned, a few Leeds supporters surrounded my friend's car. They became aggressive and started rocking the vehicle. I was sure they were going to turn the car over so I told my friend to get his foot down quick. He sped off like a racing driver. It really is very sad because, coming from Halifax, I watched Leeds play many times, and my hero was John Charles. Yet twice I have been attacked at their ground. There are countless fantastic people among the hundreds of thousands that fill English football grounds every week - and just a handful that, well, can you explain why they do what they do?

17.

The Hidden Agenda

TO BECOME A PROFESSIONAL FOOTBALLER is a privilege. To be involved in football as long as I have been is wonderful. To become a top player, and play for top teams, and then to play international football - that is a dream come true. However, in this day and age there is a hidden problem.

A recent development in English football is the formation of academies at a lot of clubs. These are designed to spot, attract and nurture young footballers, eventually turning them into first-team players. It makes enormous sense for the clubs - and has done a lot of boys a lot of good - but there is one regulation involved which parents must understand and be familiar with.

There is a serious hidden agenda. There are considerable potential dangers to the signing and binding of a boy to a professional club.

As soon as a boy signs for a professional club at the age of nine, a price is on his head. If a nine-year-old had signed for Rochdale then developed quickly and wanted to go to Manchester United, he could not just leave Rochdale to make the switch. A fee would be involved. Is that right when England international Sol Campbell can, assuming he is out of a contract, leave Spurs for nothing when he is 25? A player worth perhaps £10 million in today's market can move for nothing but a boy of nine has a fee on his head. A young boy could find it harder to leave one club and go to another than a player in his mid-twenties.

Many parents ask me for advice when a professional club wants to sign their boy. I tell them to think carefully before they do anything. It is a big decision that they are facing. For the parents of a young footballer, choosing the right club is as important as choosing the right school for their child. I warn them that there is a hidden agenda because many parents, quite understandably, are not aware of, or don't understand, the regulations. To be fair to the Football Association they attempt to keep people informed. There is nothing secret about the way the rules and regulations work but they can be difficult to take in.

If the parents of a boy fully understand the contract they are signing, and they are completely happy to sign, then that is fine. If they want to stay at the club of their choice for a long time, that is excellent, and no-one should try to entice the boy away. Trouble arrives when the boy does not like the club he signs for but the club likes him and wants to retain him as a potential first-team player.

If the boy is determined to leave the club and join another one, and the two clubs involved can't agree a fee, the Football League appeals committee becomes involved. A fee is agreed and then the club that wants to take the boy on board has to decide if they can afford the boy, or whether they think the boy is worth the fee involved.

As far as compensation goes, a club losing a player to another club is entitled to compensation if:

A) In the case of a player signed by another club as a student: Registration previously held and student offered retention, or student offered a scholarship. A scholarship is involved when a player leaves school. A scholarship is for three years, with a two years option on the side of the club. There is no freedom to move. If he moves there

**Receiving a presentation for services to the
Lancashire League from Manchester United legend
Bobby Charlton.**

Bobby has always been enthusiastic about youth development at
Old Trafford, often turning up to watch the youngsters play.

Above: The 'Class of 92' in their younger days, and below, the same lads on the greatest night of their careers.

The Theatre of Dreams

My home from home for 20 years.

Two Manchester United greats, Eric Cantona and Peter Schmeichel. They were amongst many foreign influences from whom I learnt a lot.

David and Victoria often get a raw deal from the press, but they're always willing to visit hospitals and children's homes whenever they're asked.

Almost as famous as my 1992 FA Youth Cup-winning side were
the team that won the trophy in 1994 (above).
Pictured below is one of the more recent youth teams at Old
Trafford, many of whom will become household names. In fact,
Wes Brown (pictured standing fourth from right) is already an
England international

Wes Brown, a star of the future

Sir Alex Ferguson
The greatest manager of all time? Of that there seems little doubt.

is a price on the boy's head.

B) In the case of a boy signed by another club as a contracted player: Registration previously held and offered scholarship, or registered on a scholarship, and either scholarship terminated at player's request or offered contract which was refused.

Sometimes a club will terminate a player's contract if the player is unhappy but that is not always the case. I remember when Les Kershaw, our Academy Director, signed Gavin McCann on schoolboy forms a few years ago. The schoolboy form was out before the Academy form and boys normally signed for a club at the age of 14. Gavin was not offered an apprenticeship at the age of 16 but he was pleased to sign for us, with his parents' blessing. Alex Ferguson and Les Kershaw took Mr and Mrs McCann and Gavin for a meal and Gavin signed that night.

The next day there was a problem because Gavin was upset and thought he had made a mistake and said he did not want to fulfil his contract. Les Kershaw tore the contract up. I must stress that it is very unusual for this to happen but Les said that he did not want any boy being unhappy at Manchester United.

I thought that was a great gesture by Les. Gavin McCann signed schoolboy forms at Everton shortly after and then went on to sign as an apprentice and finally as a pro. He was transferred to Sunderland shortly after that and has played many times for Sunderland's first team.

If agreement on a level of compensation cannot be reached by the the clubs then again the Football League appeals committee becomes involved. The commitee, headed by an independant chairman, includes representatives of the League Managers Association and the Professional Footballers Association.

These are the factors involved in determining the amount of compensation:

* The status of the two clubs.
* The age of the player.

* The amount of any previous compensation.
* The length of time registered.
* The terms of contract(s).
* The playing record.
* Any interest shown by other clubs.
* Costs of operating the Academy or Centre of Excellence.
* Any other cost attributable to training and development.

Academy to Academy transfers guarantee a £400,000 initial fee then £1 million additional fee based on appearances, £2,500,000 for first full cap plus percentage of transfer profit. Not long ago, a boy called Jermaine Defoe moved from Charlton Athletic, as a schoolboy, to West Ham as a scholar and contract player. Charlton received an initial £400,000 and can anticpate further payments of £250,000 after five first-team appearances, £250,000 after fifteen appearances, £250,000 after twenty-five appearances, £250,000 after first England appearance, and 15% of any future excess. Even after a career spent in youth football I find the regulations complicated, so how do parents cope?

As a club, Manchester United love to sign English boys but can you wonder when we sometimes go abroad for young talent. If we sign a boy from abroad, on many occasions you just have to pay up the boy's contract and nothing else. English boys could be priced out of the market by the demand of transfer-fee plus contract. I wonder if, one day, parents may go to court to challenge the system. It is called freedom of choice.

18.

Helping Sparky light the Welsh fire

THE IMPORTANCE OF A COMPETENT COACH should not be underestimated. Under a disorganised coach, a team has no chance at all of playing well-organised football.

I always tell coaches to look at themselves first then look at the players. Even if you do not have the best technical players in the league in which you play, you can get your players to work as hard, get stuck in, and be as well-organised as any other. You may not be as successful as a team packed with world-class players, but you can be as well-organised.

An understanding of tactics is vital. Usually a match report on the opposition is available, or better still, the coach will have been to watch forthcoming opposition wherever possible. To just tell your team not to worry about how the opposition play is arrogant. Respect the opposition but never be afraid of them - that is my motto.

Monitoring the opposition in advance does not always work, of course, because they may spring a surprise. A good coach and manager is always on the lookout for different styles and ploys. What happens if they play four at the back, five in midfield and one up front? Who picks up the spare midfield player? Who breaks from midfield? Even experienced international defenders can have a problem with this scenario. Remember the 1980 FA Cup final when West Ham manager John Lyall totally confused Arsenal's experienced back-four by withdrawing Stuart Pearson into a midfield role and playing David Cross in a lone role up front. Arsenal's defence had spare men while in midfield they were outnumbered.

It is the manager or coach's job to sort these problems out. If they can't sort them out they deserve the sack. The best bosses can react to situations immediately when they arise during matches - when the afore-mentioned surprise is sprung, a substition is made or, perhaps, caused by an injury to one's own team - and put solutions in place straight away.

In my role as assistant manager of Wales, it is vitally important for me to be able to understand the tactics of the international teams we are playing. I was thrilled when Mark Hughes, having just been appointed manager, asked me to be his assistant. I was Mark's boss when he was in Manchester United's youth team and now he is mine.

It's early days but Sparky, as he has always been known, has impressed me enormously. His knowledge of the game is vast. He has enjoyed a long and varied career and has learned a lot. Clearly, he has listened carefully to a lot of the fine coaches under whom he has worked. He has had a wonderful education at Manchester United, Barcelona, Bayern Munich, Chelsea, Southampton, Everton and Blackburn Rovers. He is a legend as a player and I sincerely hope he becomes a legend as a manager.

Mark has unbelievable passion for his beloved Wales and that is a great motivating factor for all the players in the squad. His team-talk before his first game as manager, a European Championship qualifier against Belarus in Minsk in 1999, was hugely passionate and left the players well aware that just to pull on a Welsh jersey was a great honour. I have known Mark for a long time but even I did not know what to expect from his first team talk. He is quite a quiet fellow off the field but a real colussos on it. It's like a different person takes over and, from that first team-talk, I could see that the same level of fighting spirit applies to his management as to his style of playing.

The Wales job is my first which involves coaching an international team and it is an exciting challenge. The players are brilliant to work with and show an excellent attitude towards training. They have a burning desire to succeed. If I have a criticism of them, it is that they don't really, genuinely believe in themselves enough. Injecting them with that self-belief is a big part of my job and we must all work together towards improving that because you cannot be successful in professional sport without confidence and great belief in yourself and your team- mates.

The players will certainly need a lot of confidence going into the World Cup qualifying games. Our group is very tough. Ukraine, Norway, Poland, Belgium, and Armenia present big obstacles for us. Ukraine have the dynamic duo - Shevchenko and Rebrov - up front. Without question two of the best strikers in the world. Norway have outstanding players. Solskjar, Flo, Berg, Iverson, Johnsen, the list goes on.

I was greatly encouraged by the players' performance against Poland in Warsaw in October 2000. The boys really showed their character to earn a point in one of the most amazing atmospheres I have ever experienced.

We played in the old Legia Warsaw stadium which is now knows as the Daewoo Stadium. About 40 minutes before the 8pm kick-off, a guy started screaming and shouting on the tannoy. I wondered what was going on but then I realised that he was whipping the crowd up into somehting approaching hysteria. The Polish supporters were going absolutely mental, which certainly gave our players something to think about. Mind you, I really enjoyed it because I have always found the hour directly before a game like being in a time warp. That hour seems like a week. These days the players have a long warm-up on the pitch before a game and while they are out there on the pitch the dressing room is a weird place to be. The physiotherapist and doctors have done their bit so they go quiet. The manager and coach are quiet because they have delivered their team-talk and have nothing much more to say. It is a strange period when you are in limbo really. You have handed responsibility fully over to the players and all you can do is wait and see how they fare. It is a time when even some of the most experienced managers and coaches, myself included, can get a bit nervous. Not many admit it though.

Before that Poland game I said to Mark Hughes; "Imagine what it is like when you are waiting to go into the ring to fight Mike Tyson." That Warsaw venue seemed a bit similar as the noise grew and grew. A wall of noise like that can be intimidating - that's why they do it of course - but it can also be exciting and uplifting for the away side. Just before our players went out we reminded them that a crowd never won a football match. I think the players got the message. We quietened the crowd very early in the game, which is always a good sign for the away team, and went on to clinch a thoroughly deserved 0-0 draw. I must add that the Polish crowd were one of the most sporting I have ever seen. They clapped all the way through the Welsh national anthem.

One thing in our favour though is the magnificent Millennium Stadium in Cardiff. I have been in many great stadia around the world but this is the best I have visited. It enjoys the advantage, of course, of being populated by the brilliant Welsh supporters. The noise they generate inside is incredible. We must use this fantastic arena and the atmosphere generated by those phenomenal fans to our advantage.

19.

Sir Alex Ferguson

WHEN ALEX FERGUSON ARRIVED at Manchester United as manager, one of his first acts was to hold a meeting with all the professional playing staff.

Apart from his assistant, Archie Knox, none of the other coaches were present. To be fair to the boss, he had already spoken to the rest of the staff, so we did not feel neglected. Being a nosy so-and-so, I was waiting outside the room when the meeting finished and I grabbed Bryan Robson and asked him what was said. Bryan's immediate response was a simple "He'll do for me."

The Boss had just told the players that he demands that they gives 100% every time they play and 100% commitment to the club. If they don't, they have no chance of remaining part of the club. Robbo's face was beaming because nobody gave more on the football field for Manchester United than Bryan Robson. It was the perfect start - and there was a lot more to come. The Boss called me into his office after a couple of weeks and told me that he thought the standard of young players at the club was not good enough. I promptly told him to get me some better players and I would produce more first team players for him. "I'll get you the best," he said. We were up and running.

The View From the Dugout

As quickly as I was elated, however, I had a big shock which threw me into a state of depression. Right out of the blue, all the morning training sessions for all the professional players, plus the apprentice professionals, were suddenly taken over by the Boss and Archie Knox. Brian Whitehouse, who was the reserve team manager, and myself stood on the touchline watching. I joked with Brian that we were the best-paid ball-boys in the country. Our only relief was that we could get our group to work with in the afternoon.

I was hurt and bewildered and decided that if this was going to be the way things were, I would have to leave the club that I love because I could not stand watching other people work with my group of young players. Fortunately this only went on for a few weeks and then I was handed my group of players back again. To this day, I have never asked the Boss why he did that.

A new era had begun. Things were happening that I had never experienced before. The Boss and Archie came to every reserve and youth team match they could attend. Unless the first team were playing, they were watching our young players. All the boys soon got the message. They realised that the boss was watching their every move. It may have been a bit intimidating for some of them because the Boss was quick to criticise any player who he thought was not giving everything but I was pleased that this was happening. Weak-kneed players are no good to Manchester United.

Everyone at the club was beginning to realise we were in the business of being successful - and staying successful. In some ways the Boss is a lot like Brian Clough. Nobody gets away with anything. Archie Knox was a big help to me. He came along to most evening training with the schoolboys and got stuck into the coaching sessions. The sessions were very lively, believe me.

Like myself, the Boss was very strong on discipline. All the rooms at the training ground had to be spotless. He would inspect all the rooms on Friday afternoons and the apprentice professionals could not go home until everything was spick and span. I now had an ally on my stance as far as alcohol with young players was concerned. I always drummed it into young players that they should not drink alcohol and now I was backed up to the hilt by the boss. The young players knew they were risking their careers if they were caught drinking.

Even though the discipline was strong, a great atmosphere was created. The Boss and the rest of the coaches would hold regular quizzes in the manager's office. All the young players were crammed into the room and some of the answers they gave were absolutely hilarious. This was serving an important role. The players realised they could relax in the company of the Boss. The manager's office used to be as busy as Manchester airport. Parents flooded in with their young sons. We were hot on the trail of talented youngsters and the Boss was the focal point. Without him we would definitely not have signed all our superb youngsters. He made the parents and their sons realise that Manchester United was the club for them. His words still ring in my ears. "Trust me," was the two words he used to the parents. He can be trusted, and I do not know of any young player who has been let down by him.

The Boss would go anywhere in the world to try and sign talented young players. I don't know of any other manager who would jump into his car or dash to the airport and fly anywhere in pursuit of a young player. How he did this and all the thousand and one other jobs that a manager has to do is beyond me. He believed that the way forward for the club was with the young players. At the time, the first team were not doing brilliantly but he had a plan and he had the courage to do it his way. Fortunately the board believed in him and gave him the time that he needed.

A lot of managers say that winning is not important for youth teams but I don't really believe them. Playing the right way, and winning, is important. I always felt that the Boss wanted his youth team and reserve team to win matches. Every Saturday morning when the first team were playing away, the phone used to go at 12.50pm in the coach's room and it was that familiar gravel-throated voice asking; how d'ye get on? It was the Boss. Normally my answer was that we had won. Great, he would say. Who played well? Then he would always say well done. Once I remember him ringing up one Saturday asking about the result and I said rather sheepishly that we had lost 2-1 to Stoke City. There was a pause, and I thought he had gone. He eventually said, that's disappointing, and our conversation fizzled out.

I admired his involvement with all the players at the club. It sent a message out to all the coaches that we had to look after the players. We had to care about each and every one because he did. We had to give them the best coaching. We had to work long hours with the players, not just on the training pitch, but off it as well. The young players learned to trust the coaches. The manager's philosophy was working.

When the youth team won the FA Youth Cup in 1992, which was the first time in almost 30 years, the Boss was on the pitch at Old Trafford celebrating the victory over Crystal Palace with myself, the rest of the youth staff and players. He had sat up in the directors' box watching the game with Cliff Butler, who is editor of the Manchester United programme. Cliff is an ardent United supporter who lives for the club, and he can certainly tell you everything about them.

Cliff told the Boss that the youth team's success could be an omen because the last time United had won the FA Youth Cup, in 1964, the first team had gone on to win the First Division championship the following year. I certainly believed that quite a few of the players who lifted the trophy in 1992 were going to lift many a trophy when playing for the first team.

Still, there was that wait for the first first-team trophy under Alex. No matter how much good work is going on, the only true measurement of success is the number of trophies in the cabinet. What a relief, and what a fantastic feeling, it was when we won the FA Cup against Crystal Palace in 1990. The rest is history. That was the beginning of many magnificent achievements. We won the lot. That night, eight years later, in Barcelona when we beat Bayern Munich to win the European Cup was just pure magic. Sir Alex Ferguson deserves to be talked of as one of the truly great managers.

Even when success flooded in at first-team level, the manager's hunger for more trophies did not diminish his desire for his youth team to be successful. For him, senior and junior success went hand in hand. I suppose you could excuse him for not taking such a massive interest in the reserves and the youth teams with the first team being so successful but that never happened. If the board of directors do not keep him at the club in some capacity when he calls it a day as manager, they will be making a big mistake. The Boss should be able to tell the Directors what job he wants. There should be no argument, because without Sir Alex Ferguson, Manchester United Football Club would not be the power they are today.

He helped me to produce some very good young players, just as I asked him to do when he arrived at Old Trafford. He, through United's wonderful scouts, gave me the material to work with. He has been a superb public relations ambassador and spent time with parents and youngsters and persuaded them that they must become part of the club. He has also kept in touch with the same youngsters and followed their progress. In return I would like to think that I have helped him produce some great Manchester United teams with the number of youngsters who have graduated to the first team and become household names and internationals.

Let me recount one incident which sums up what his dedication and influence has been like. One of the Christmas games of 1998 was against Middlesborough at Old Trafford. On the night before the game, Jim Ryan, the reserve team coach who was working with the first team at that time, rang me to tell me that there had been a death in the manager's family. His sister-in-law had passed away, so could I change my plans and come to the game to give him a hand because the Boss would not be there. Naturally, I said yes, and early on the Saturday morning, the Boss rang and asked me to help Jim. I was very touched that he made time to phone me when he had more important things on his mind but that is just the type of man who never takes anyone for granted.

The game was a complete disaster for United, who lost one of their rare home games. The final score was 3-2 and at one stage we were three goals down. The crowd were getting very angry and one thought crossed my mind. It was that I would not like to be the next manager of Manchester United. How do you follow such a class act as Sir Alex Ferguson?

20.

The special grounds

JUST BEFORE CHRISTMAS 1999 I had the great privilege and pleasure of helping out Bury Football Club. Neil Warnock had just left to manage Sheffield United and Bury were left with no manager and no first-team coach. Their chairman, Terry Robinson, and Neville Neville, the commercial manager, asked me to help coach the first team. Two players, Andy Preece and Steve Redmond, were appointed joint-managers and they had the arduous task of playing and managing. I worked with Andy, Steve and the players for two weeks and I loved every minute of it. However, it saddened me to witness a very famous club, and a super football club, being in such serious financial trouble.

Professional footballers are resilient blokes. The ones at Bury have to be because before we could start training, the youth team coach Alex Jones had to shovel dog muck off the playing area. The training facilities are very poor but that did not deter the players from showing great enthusiasm and good skills in their training session. I was very pleased with their efforts and, although two weeks is a short stint, I got to know all the coaching staff and the players well and I wish them well in the future. Terry Robinson and Neville Neville, not forgetting Jill Neville who is the secretary and Neville's wife, are great people and they love Bury FC so much.

United's reserves play their home games at Bury and if I had my way Manchester United would take over Bury and let Terry Robinson have a good night's sleep. Tell that to the Football Association and they would throw it out, thinking United had an ulterior motive. But why, with all the vast amounts of money about at the top level in football, do clubs like Bury have to struggle so much?

It is extremely difficult for lower division clubs to keep going and I admire them tremendously. There are a million wonderful stories and one of them always brings a smile to my face when it comes to mind.

When I was at Barrow in the old Fourth Division some of the journeys we had to make were mind-boggling. The journey I dreaded most of all was Torquay United. A night match at Torquay was horrendous because there was no question of stopping overnight in a hotel - we travelled all the way up from Devon to Cumbria straight after the game.

This particular match we had done well (we had won a corner I think) and our manager Don McEvoy, who was a great bloke, said that we could have a drink after the match. For footballeras, especially in the 1960s, that was licence to kill. We stopped at a hotel on the way and got well and truly oiled and, not satisfied with that, took a load of bottles onto the coach where the surprise party continued with a sing-song. Mind you, Torquay to Barrow without today's motorways is one hell of a trek so we reckoned we deserved a drink or two.

I finally walked - well, staggered - up my driveway at 6am. My next-door neighbour was just coming down the drive, on his way to work at Vickers shipyard as I made my way in. He could not believe I was just coming home and came up to me and whispered, "Have you been out with a bird Eric?" I burst out laughing and held up my hands: "Just getting home from work."

I have been fortunate to travel a lot and visit some fabulous stadia. I have also been to other grounds which are falling to pieces and yet most of them have their own charm and appeal and their own set of people, just as devoted as any in football, determined to keep their clubs going.

My four favourite grounds are Old Trafford, Goodison Park, the Millennium Stadium in Cardiff and the Nou Camp Stadium in Barcelona.

Old Trafford has always been a very special place and now the stadium is absolutely magnificent. After a few problems with the pitch it is now in great shape and certainly one of the best in the country thanks to the excellent work of Keith Kent and the rest of his groundstaff. It is so important to have a good surface, especially if you have a good footballing team. When I joined United in 1981 I told Peter Solski, who looked after the Cliff training ground, that if he produced a good surface I would be able to get the young players to produce top class football on it. Pete duly did that and, after he left, Ben Styles carried on the good work. Now Old Trafford has got the good surface it needs and deserves. The Theatre of Dreams must have a perfect stage.

Goodison Park will always mean a great deal to me. I have terrific memories of the place stretching back to 1972 when, just after I joined, every Friday afternoon I took the apprentices to Goodison from the Bellefield training ground to clean the boots of the first-team players in preparation for the next day's match.

There were no kit men in those days of course. The coach was responsible for packing all the kit and we had to be spot on with everything. I even unscrewed all the boots in all the studs just to make sure that, come Saturday afternoon at 2pm, when the players were getting changed, none of them got into a panic by discovering one of the studs in his boots had got stuck.

Every Friday afternoon, when I had finished all my duties, I walked down the Goodison Park tunnel - from where next day the likes of Gordon West and Joe Royle would emerge to the mightiest of roars - and walk onto the hallowed pitch. I would just look round at the huge stands and terraces and enjoy the wonderful feeling standing on that famous turf and gazing round that magnificent stadium.

It was all such a far cry from travelling round the old Fourth Division grounds with Barrow and Hartlepool to places like Chester, where we had to climb through a hole in the wall to get to the bath. We could only take baths four at a time because it was so small! Now, glorious Goodison Park was my workplace. Already I realised how lucky I was - if only I had known what was to come!

The Nou Camp Stadium is a fantastic arena which was elevated to even greater heights for everyone associated with Manchester United by that famous day in May 1999. While most of the top grounds have a lot of history to them, however, the Millennium Stadium in Cardiff provides proof that with the architectural expertise available nowadays a brand new ground can be built with instant greatness.

The Millennium Stadium is awesome. The first time I walked in there with Mark Hughes and the Welsh players it took my breath away. The design is fantastic and it is a stunning sight empty so we wondered what it would be like with a full house of nearly 75,000 people inside. We had all seen the games there in the 1999 rugby World Cup on television and they were truly memorable so we could not wait to play there. Our first game was a friendly against Finland - not the sort of fixture you would expect to be a huge draw - but we got our wish of playing in front of a full house. What a wonderful experience.

Yes, wonderful. But then when I look back there have been so many great days and I owe them all to the great institution that is football. From the days carrying that blanket round the pitch for the brass band at Turf Moor, to joining in the celebrations when Manchester United lifted the Champions Cup to complete the treble in the Nou Camp. I have enjoyed every minute.

This book was produced by The Parrs Wood Press, a specialist sports publishing company based in Manchester.

For a free catalogue of books by The Parrs Wood Press write to:

The Parrs Wood Press
FREEPOST
Manchester M15 9PW
(no stamp required)

or email: sport@parrswoodpress.com

www.parrswoodpress.com